CHINA WITHOUT MAO

CHINA WITHOUT MAO

The Search for a New Order

Immanuel C. Y. Hsü

OXFORD UNIVERSITY PRESS

Oxford   New York   Toronto   Melbourne

1982

Oxford University Press
Oxford London Glasgow
New York Toronto Melbourne
Nairobi Dar es Salaam Cape Town
Kuala Lumpur Singapore Hong Kong
Tokyo Delhi Calcutta Madras Karachi

and associate companies in
Beirut Berlin Ibadan Mexico City

LIBRARY OF CONGRESS CATALOGING IN PUBLICATION DATA

Hsü, Immanuel Chung-yueh, 1923–
  China without Mao.

  Bibliography: p.
  Includes index.
  1. China—Politics and government—1976–
I. Title.
DS779.26.H77   951.05'7   82–2161
ISBN 0–19–503133–4   AACR2
ISBN 0–19–503134–2 (pbk.)

Printing (last digit) 9 8 7 6 5 4 3

Printed in the United States of America

For
K. C. Liu

Preface

After Mao, the deluge?

To many, Mao was the personification of Chinese communism, and China without Mao seemed inconceivable. Yet there has been no "deluge," no chaos, but rather the gradual emergence of a pragmatic new order with a different approach to socialist transformation. This new order grew out of a critical reassessment of China's new historical mission and represents a rejection of the Maoist methods.

During the last decade of his life, Mao Zedong attempted to reach the peak of revolution through the gigantic social and political upheaval of the Cultural Revolution. He sought ideological purity through intensified class struggle and the purge of high party and government leaders and intellectuals. Though in appearance an endeavor of noble idealism, the Cultural Revolution ushered in a decade of destruction and disorder. The party was decimated. Industry, agriculture, and science suffered severe losses. Disruption in education left a generation untrained, and scholars were denied years of teaching and research, resulting in an incalculable loss of human resources. Ironically, the Cultural Revolution turned out to be anticultural.

It is significant that the purge of senior party members made way for the rise of Mao's wife, Jiang Qing, who catapulted to the position of first vice-chairman of the Central Cultural Revolutionary Committee in 1966. She built up a radical following which together with the military under Lin Biao become the chief beneficiary of the Cultural Revolution. When Lin was killed following an abortive coup in September 1971, Jiang Qing rose further in national politics. At the Tenth Party Congress in 1973, she and three senior associates—Wang Hongwen, Zhang Chunqiao, and Yao Wenyuan—won leadership positions. With Premier Zhou Enlai and Chairman Mao both in ill health, Jiang Qing's group prepared themselves for succession. Mao patronized them but also warned them not to become a "Gang of Four." With the support of Kang Sheng's secret police, they tyrannized the country. Perceptive leaders were appalled at this state of affairs yet dared not speak out for fear of reprisal.

The death of Mao marked an epochal turning point in Chinese politics. The struggle for succession that ensued led to the smashing of the Gang and the emergence of Hua Guofeng, Mao's "anointed successor," as party chairman and state premier. But Hua was soon challenged by surviving victims of the Cultural Revolution under the leadership of Deng Xiaoping, the deposed former vice-premier. Termed pragmatists, the new leaders question the value of the Cultural Revolution and of Mao's policies of continous class struggle and uninterrupted revolution. They doubt the efficacy of Mao's economic adventurism, which during his twenty-seven-year rule failed to lift China from poverty and backwardness.

These progmatists vow that the Cultural Revolution must never be allowed to recur. They advocate unity, stability, discipline, and greater domestic liberty and international cooperation. Most important, they have launched a program of modernization under a younger leadership and tried to stimulate enthusiasm for work through material incentives. Deng's "Economics in Command" has replaced Mao's "Politics in Command." The adoption of the principle, "From each according to his ability, to each according to his work," reflects the new emphasis on expertise. Foreign-trained intellectuals, despised in the past, are now cherished as patriots. With these new policies, the pragmatists hope to render their nation a powerful, prosperous, highly cultured, and advanced socialist state by the year 2000.

The pragmatists gained power at the expense of Hua and the Maoists. Their crowning victory came in June 1981 when the Sixth Plenary Session of the Eleventh Central Committee officially affirmed socialist economic development as the central task of the party and government under the new collective leadership of party Chairman Hu Yaobang, Vice-Chairman Deng Xiaoping, and Premier Zhao Ziyang. The Cultural Revolution was completely repudiated, and Mao was held chiefly responsible for its excesses, while the party assessed itself a fair share of guilt for not having prevented his mistakes.

Public reaction to the new policies is overwhelmingly positive. Long stifled under the strict regimentation of Mao, the people yearned for civil and economic liberalization, and they have gradually come alive to the new order. For all their respect for the Great Helmsman, his passing was in many ways a relief, slowly lifting the heavy burden of omnipresent politics from their shoulders. They welcome the changes.

However, despite public support of the new leadership, the pragmatists' victory remains incomplete. Of its 38 million members, about half joined the party and rose to positions of responsibility during the Cultural Revolutionary decade. This large group's indifferent attitude toward the new policies has prompted the expression "The two ends are hot, but the middle is cold." Unless this pivotal group is won over or reformed, progress toward modernization will be compromised.

Recent changes in China must not lead to mistaken assumptions about a radical transformation in the nature of the Chinese state. Rather, they signify a shift of approach within the framework of the Chinese communist system. China remains committed to the four basic principles of the socialist line, the proletarian dictatorship, the leadership of the Communist party, and Marxism-Leninism and the Thought of Mao. Still, with the Sixth Plenary Session's rejection of Maoist class struggle and Mao's adventurous economic policies, and with the adoption of a more realistic modernization program, a new order has emerged, and the Maoist era is ended.

Writing contemporary history one lacks the benefit of hindsight and perspective that the study of earlier history affords. The importance of the time dimension in historical judgments is obvious; short-term assessments are perforce tentative. To offset the tendency to subjectivity, the author conducted field research in China in 1979, 1980, and 1981. He lectured at the Beijing, Fudan, and Nanjing Universities and held discussions with many persons in various walks of life. He gained the distinct feeling that China is making progress as the effects of the New Order begin to manifest themselves. However, modernizations will continue to be slow and labored, and it would be unrealistic to expect more than moderate progress in the next decade or two.

✻   ✻   ✻

A word about the methods of romanizing Chinese characters seems in order. I follow the principle of using the system generally accepted in the geopolitical region of reference. Thus, in reference to mainland China the Pinyin phonetic system is used, and in reference to Taiwan, the Wade-Giles system. Though this requires familiarity with more than one system, it should cause the least confusion in identification of people, places, and literary works (see the guide provided in the back of the book).

In preparing this book I have received valuable help from my research assistants, Cathleen Costa and Eugene Y. C. Lau. To them and to my typist Alice Kladnik, I wish to extend my deep appreciation. I am also indebted to Professors K. C. Liu, Stephen and Eloise Hay, and Charles Litzinger for various comments and suggestions. Responsibility for the final content, however, rests solely with the author.

I. C. Y. Hsü

Santa Barbara, Calif.
December 4, 1981

Contents

1 The Smashing of the Gang of Four   3

The Deaths of National Leaders   4
The Gang of Four   12
Mao and the Gang   22

2 Deng Xiaoping and China's New Order   29

Deng's Rehabilitation   30
Deng's Drive for Political Dominance   33
The Demystification of Mao   44

3 The Normalization of Relations between China
and the United States   56

The Normalization of Diplomatic Relations   58
The Normalization of Trade and Other Relations   78

4 The Four Modernizations   91

The Ten-Year Plan   93
Major Problems of Modernization: Capital, Manpower
and Planning   101

Retrenchment and Revised Priorities   106
Profit, Material Incentive, and Structural
Reorganization   110
The Consequences of Rapid Modernization   112
Foreign Value and Chinese Essence   116

5 The End of the Maoist Age   126

The Trial of the Gang of Four
and the Lin Biao Group   126
Assessments of Mao   142
A New Leadership and a New Order   156
Chinese Communism: A Thirty-Year Review   158

6 Taiwan's "Economic Miracle" and the Prospect
for Unification with Mainland China   172

Causes of Taiwan's Economic Success   173
The Prospect for Reunification   179

Guide to Pinyin and Wade-Giles Systems   187

Appendix: On Questions of Party History   191

Index   205

CHINA WITHOUT MAO

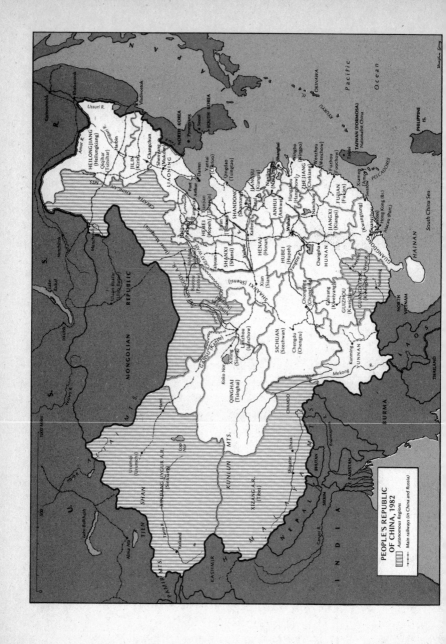

PEOPLE'S REPUBLIC
OF CHINA, 1982

░░░ Autonomous Regions
+—+—+ Main railways (in China and Russia)

1

The Smashing of the Gang of Four

Nineteen seventy-six was a year of agony for China. Deep bereavement was felt in every corner of the land over the loss of three of its great leaders: Premier Zhou Enlai in January, Marshal Zhu De in July, and Chairman Mao Zedong in September. Added to human grief was a series of natural disasters; in July a major earthquake demolished the industrial city of Tangshan, 105 miles southeast of Beijing (Peking), and during the next two months the Yellow River flooded seven times. Compounding the human misery and political instability was the succession crisis precipitated by Mao's wife Jiang Qing and her associates, later dubbed the Gang of Four. Indeed, the tumultuous year was marked by what the Chinese call "natural disaster and human misfortune" (*tianzai renhuo*). It was a time of sorrow, yet like darkness before dawn, also a time of hope. Out of disorder a new order was struggling to be born, and with it was the promise of greater stability, progress, and a better life for the people.

THE DEATHS OF NATIONAL LEADERS

Zhou Enlai (1898–1976)

The death of Zhou Enlai on January 8, 1976, was an irreparable loss. A pillar of strength in both party and government, he was the moderating influence through numerous political storms. Zhou had saved the country from the utter chaos during the upheaval of the Cultural Revolution and had helped thwart the Gang of Four's grasp for supreme power.

Born to a gentry family of Shaohsing toward the end of the Qing dynasty, Zhou attended the Nankai University Middle School before going to Japan for further studies. In 1920 he went to France as a worker-study student and spent the next four years in Europe, where he, along with fellow-student Deng Xiaoping, joined the Chinese Communist Youth Corps and later the Chinese Communist Party. He became a loyal supporter of Mao after the Zunyi Conference of January 1935. As premier from 1949 until his death, Zhou submitted to Mao's oracular leadership, running the machinery of government unobtrusively while quietly moderating certain of Mao's excesses.

Zhou exuded a disarming charm and an urbane sophistication. His savvy manner and vast knowledge of world affairs struck all foreign visitors. Dag Hammarskjold, the late United Nations secretary-general, considered him "the superior brain I have so far met in the field of foreign politics." President Nixon said: "Only a handful of men in the twentieth century will ever match Premier Zhou's impact on world history. . . . None surpass him in keen intellect, philosophical breadth and the experienced wisdom which made him a great leader."[1]

Afflicted with cancer as early as 1972, Zhou appears to have engineered the rehabilitation of Deng Xiaoping in 1973 as vice-premier and groomed him for succession. In response, the radicals launched the Anti-Lin Biao Anti-Confucius Campaign to harass Zhou by allusion. Zhou continued to work even following his hospitalization in the summer of 1974, administering

Zhou Enlai, one of his last official portraits.

state affairs from his sickbed, receiving visitors, and making occasional public appearances. He attended the celebration of the twenty-fifth anniversary of the founding of the People's Republic and delivered the keynote speech at the Fourth National People's Congress in January 1975. This speech laid the groundwork for what has since become known as the Four

Modernizations: a comprehensive modernization of agriculture, industry, national defense, and science and technology that would put China in the front ranks of the world by the end of the century.

Dead at seventy-eight, Zhou was mourned by his 900 million countrymen as a beloved elder-protector, hero both in the struggle of revolution and in the management of the affairs of state. He must be credited for long years of invaluable service to the state, especially during the "decade of catastrophe" otherwise known as the Cultural Revolution.

The Emergence of Hua Guofeng

Zhou had carefully groomed Deng Xiaoping to be his successor. In the last year of Zhou's hospitalization, Deng had amassed considerable power and was the de facto premier directing the day-to-day work of the State Council and receiving foreign leaders. Yet, shortly after eulogizing Zhou at the memorial service on January 15, 1976, Deng dropped out of sight without explanation, and on February 6 the *Renmin Ribao* [People's daily] carried a front page article attacking the "unrepentent" powerholders who took the "capitalist road." The Cultural Revolutionary group under Jiang Qing were promoting Zhang Chunqiao, second vice-premier, for the premiership, but Zhang was unacceptable to many party seniors and military leaders. On February 7 the Chinese government announced the startling appointment of Hua Guofeng, the sixth-ranking vice-premier and minister of public security, as acting premier. This choice pleased neither the radicals nor the moderates but was not challenged due to Mao's enormous prestige.

In the waning months of his life, Mao, under pressure from his wife, had wanted to favor the Cultural Revolutionary Group but hesitated to offend the senior cadres and military leaders. In this dilemma, Mao appears to have selected Hua, a faithful follower who was ideologically safe and who would adequately serve the state until Jiang Qing's group could assume power. The choice of Hua, a former party first secretary in Mao's home province of Hunan and an agricultural expert, was clearly a compromise as he had close ties with neither the pragmatists nor the radicals. At the same time, in naming Hua, Mao masterfully blocked Zhou's scheme to place Deng in line for succession.

Hua had no power base of his own. In domestic politics he moved cautiously, creating friendships with senior cadres and military leaders and avoiding making enemies in the Politburo. This calculated stance won the approbation of Mao but the enmity of Jiang Qing and Zhang Chunqiao. A member of their writing team, using the nom de plume Liang Xiao (meaning two schools, i.e. Beijing and Qinghua Universities) wrote a historical allegory, "A Second Evaluation of Confucius," to attack the one "who assumed the position of Acting Prime Minister in the capacity of grand duke."[2]

Shortly after Hua's appointment, a momentous event took place during the Qingming Festival, when the Chinese traditionally visit the ancestral tombs. Between March 29 and April 4, an increasing number of people went daily to Tian An Men Square to pay tribute to the late Premier Zhou and to lay

Tomb of the Unknown Soldier in Tian An Men Square, Beijing.

wreaths at the Monument to the Martyrs of the Revolution, which had become the symbolic tomb of Zhou. When the wreaths were removed by police and security guards, people were enraged. On April 5, 100,000 gathered at Tian An Men Square in a protest demonstration chanting "the era of Qin Shih Huang is gone," hoisting signs in support of Deng, and singing the praises of Zhou and Deng while criticizing Mao by allusion.[3] Emotion soon reached a feverish pitch, and the demonstration got out of control. Frenzied demonstrators set fire to four motorcars and smashed the windows of a military barrack before they were dispersed by police, security guards, and militiamen.

Mayor Wu De of Beijing linked the violent outburst with the opponents of the "Antirightist Deviationist Campaign." Deng was openly accused of being a ringleader, a capitalist roader, and "the general behind-the-scene promoter of the Rightist Deviationist attempt to reverse correct verdicts." Two days later (April 7) on Mao's recommendation, the Central Committee ordered Deng, "whose problem has turned into one of antagonistic contradictions," dismissed from all party and government posts, but allowed him to "keep his party membership so as to see how he will behave himself in the future."

Meanwhile, the appointment of Hua as premier and first vice-chairman of the party was announced.[4] On April 8, 100,000 people paraded in Tian An Men Square in a counterdemonstration to support the new leadership. Hua emerged as the dark horse winner in the succession struggle for the premiership.

On April 30 Mao gave Hua three crucial handwritten instructions: (1) "Carry out the work slowly, not in haste"; (2) "Act according to past principles"; and (3) "With you in charge, I am at ease."[5] Viewing the instructions as implying Mao's intention to designate him his heir, Hua forwarded the first two to the Poliburo in the presence of an infuriated Gang of Four, who now considered him no longer a possible ally but a new enemy. Zhang Chunqiao, who coveted the premiership, indicated through the writer Liang Xiao that the chairman's messages might have been fabricated. Hua remained throughout unperturbed, keeping secret the third instruction and reserving it for future use.

The Tangshan Earthquake

As if the deaths of national leaders and the political confusion of the succession struggle were not enough punishment for the country, a gigantic earthquake measuring 8.2 on the Richter scale occurred on July 28, 1976, in Tangshan, a mining center of 1.6 million inhabitants. It leveled the entire city and caused considerable damage to the nearby metropolis of Tianjin, China's third largest city with a population of 4.3 million. Even Beijing felt the tremors and suffered minor damage. Tangshan itself was reduced to a desert of rubble. A confidential government report listed 655,237 dead and 779,000 injured, although later figures given by the Chinese Seismology Society were considerably lower.[6] Premier Hua remarked that the destruction and loss of lives were on a scale "rarely seen in history." Following tradition the Chinese people viewed such massive natural disasters as portents of social and political upheaval: what more could the people and state survive?

Mao Zedong (1893–1976)

For years Mao had been afflicted with Parkinson's disease, a slowly degenerative sickness causing muscular rigidity and tremors. His health failed rapidly in the last two or three years of his life due to a stroke which affected the left side of his body impairing his speech. Each day moments of clarity and well-being alternated with lapse into a less lucid state, hence the strange meeting times and abrupt notices given to foreign dignitaries who awaited audiences with him.

When President Gerald Ford visited China in early December 1975, he was summoned to Mao's residence with only minutes' notice. The chairman walked with some difficulty but carried on the interview for an hour and fifty minutes, having some trouble with his speech but able to express himself in writing. Although the picture of Mao and Ford released by the Chinese government showed the chairman in remarkably good shape, four weeks later on December 31 when another American[7] saw him at midnight and on instant notice, Mao looked tired, worn, old, and lonely.

The deterioration of Mao's health accelerated after the New Year, and by June 1976 he could no longer receive foreign visitors. Everybody knew that the end was drawing near, but when death actually came on September 9 it shook the world—not because it was unexpected, but rather because it was so final, so momentous—the man whom the Chinese called their "sun" had fallen. Eulogies came from all over the world. British Prime Minister James Callaghan said: "He will be remembered as a man of great vision and as a thinker with a profound sense of history. China's position in the world of today is a memorial to his unique achievement." President Ford said: "It is tragic that a man of this great remarkable ability, skill, vision, and foresight has passed away."[8] The world had lost a towering figure, and 900 million Chinese, the hero of their revolution.

A full assessment of Mao must wait until history has had time to digest his impact on China and the world; for now, only preliminary remarks are in order. For China, Mao was Lenin and Stalin combined. He was a great revolutionary, the most successful of the mid-twentieth century. His greatest achievement was the seizure of power through the creative adaptation of Marxist-Leninist theory to the realities of the situation in China. Influenced by Li Dazhao, he came to believe in the liberation of the peasant as the prelude to the liberation of China. He evolved the strategy of organizing the peasantry to encircle the cities and created a successful model of revolution for the Third World. He envisioned the ultimate application of this strategy to the international scene, urging the Third World to unite, engulf, and effect the eventual downfall of the Western bourgeois societies.

Throughout his life, Mao was motivated by a perpetual restlessness. He rebelled against his father, against landlord and capitalist, against Nationalist rule, against Soviet domination and revisionism, and finally against his own party estab-

Official portrait of Mao Zedong.

lishment and senior associates. Impatient for change, he wanted to transform the state, the society, and human nature in one stroke—"Ten thousand years are too long; seize the day, seize the hour!" A purist at heart, he kept up the momentum of revolution by creating incessant upheaval, exhausting both country and people. Much national energy was spent on mass movement and internecine strife, which impeded national progress. His twenty-seven-year rule brought little improvement in people's living standard.

It thus appears that after the success of revolution in 1949, the genius that was in Mao was largely spent. The ingredients that led him to the seizure of power could not lead him to successfully administer the sprawling state. After the first years of liberation, Mao's leadership faltered. The Antirightist·Campaign (1957) did irreparable damage to the intellectuals whose knowledge and skills China sorely needed. The rush to commune was too hasty; the Great Leap Forward went backward; the fight with Peng Dehuai was ill-conceived; and the decimation of the party during the Cultural Revolution was an unmitigated disaster. The fostering of Jiang Qing as a national leader and possible successor worked against the wishes of the people and Mao's senior associates. In his last years Mao spun himself farther and farther into a cocoon of his own making, insensitive to the feelings of the masses he had always claimed to represent. He died a lonely and unhappy man, his dream of transforming human nature and turning China into a powerful modern state unfulfilled. Historical perspective will in due time allow a full assessment of Mao's achievements and mistakes. For now, my own view of his life may be summed up in the following words:

As a revolutionary,
   Mao had few peers.
As a nation-builder,
   He was unequal to the task.

革命有餘
建國不足

THE GANG OF FOUR

The Plot of the Gang

The absence of a constitutional mechanism for the peaceful transfer of power led to a succession crisis when the incumbent leader died. The intense power struggle that erupted following

Mao's death was led by his wife, Jiang Qing, who aspired to succeed him as chairman, to make Wang Hongwen chairman of the Standing Committee of the National People's Congress, and to install Zhang Chunqiao premier of the State Council. Yao Wenyuan, already in charge of the party's propaganda department, was probably to be designated a "cultural tzar" with added titles. These four, the hard core of the Cultural Revolutionary Group, conspired to seize power, but their major obstacle was Hua Guofeng. As the first vice-chairman of the party, premier of the State Council, and the object of Mao's instruction ("With you in charge, I am at ease"), Hua had a firm claim to succession. Hua also had the support of Wang Dongxing, Mao's chief bodyguard and head of the 20,000-man 8341 special unit.

Jiang Qing's trump card, Mao, was gone. Still in her deck were control of the media and of the urban militia in key places such as Shanghai, Beijing, Tianjin, Shenyang, and Guangzhou.[9] Before Mao's death the Four had schemed to distribute weapons and ammunition to the Shanghai militia, establishing a sort of National General Militia Headquarters to rival the Military Commission in Beijing. The day after Mao's death, six million rounds of ammunition were issued to the Shanghai militia.[10]

Jiang Qing received additional military support from Mao's nephew, Mao Yuanxin, political commissar of the Shenyang Military Region. He organized a 10,000-man task force in preparation for a march on Beijing to support Jiang Qing's planned coup. He was also seen in Baoding trying to bring about the disaffection of the 38th regiment and in Tangshan attempting to enlist support from army units sent there for earthquake relief work.[11]

In spite of this support, the Jiang Qing faction remained weak militarily due to the militia's lack of firepower and good commanders. To compensate, Jiang Qing tried to recruit two militarily powerful Politburo members—General Chen Xilian (commander of the Beijing Military Region) and Su Zhenhua (political commissar of the navy). Both men informed Hua of these approaches.[12] The Four had tried earlier to elicit support from Marshal Zhu De, only to be rejected and ridiculed.[13] Thus, while the Gang of Four dominated media and education, they were unable to increase substantially their military power.

The senior party cadres and military leaders, who loathed Jiang Qing and her cohorts but had been powerless against them as long as Mao lived, decided secretly after the Tian An Men Square Incident that only a countercoup could stop the Four from seizing power. They entrusted to Ye Jianying, minister of defense, the delicate task of cultivating friendship with Hua and of promising him their support as Mao's successor.[14] Hua knew only too well the Gang's record and ambitions.

Another anti-Jiang Qing force was also in secret operation. Deng Xiaoping, dismissed in April and hunted by the Gang, had fled to Canton under the protection of Ye Jianying and Xu Shiyou. These three, in a secret meeting also attended by several others including Zhao Ziyang (now premier) decided to fight the Four by forming an alliance with the Fuzhou and Nanjing Military Regions, with headquarters in Guangzhou. Should Jiang Qing gain power, they would establish a rival provisional Central Committee to contest her. After Mao's death Deng secretly returned to Beijing to await developments.[15]

The Gang meanwhile were plotting to assassinate Politburo members, with Hua, Ye, and several others as the main targets. Facing a common threat, the two became close allies and made the necessary preparations for a coup, which included the winning over of Wang Dongxing. A three-way coalition thus formed, with Ye as the mastermind, Hua laying out the plan of action, and Wang implementing it. Shanghai would be secured first; and for this purpose the help of General Xu Shiyou of the Guangzhou Military Region, who had extensive connections in the Shanghai-Nanjing area, was enlisted to obtain the cooperation of the Shanghai garrison commander and win control of the key city *before* the urban militia could act.[16] In Beijing, Hua had the firm support of Commander Chen Xilian, Mayor Wu De, and the cooperation of the garrison forces, the army, and special unit 8341.

The "Deathbed Adjuration"

During the mourning period, Jiang Qing appeared more pre-occupied with succession than grief. Soon after Mao's death she went to the General Office of the Central Committee (under Wang Dongxing) and obliged the secretary on duty to hand over a batch of Mao's documents. Only after Hua's personal intercession did she reluctantly return them, and then only after two of the documents had been tampered with. Hua ordered all of Mao's papers sealed. The two altered pieces were:[17]

1. A June 3, 1976, document of Mao's meeting with Politburo members including Hua, Ye, Wang Hongwen, and Zhang Chunqiao, at which time Mao allegedly told them: "From now on you should help Jiang Qing carry the Red Banner. Don't let it fall. You should alert her against committing the errors she has committed." That such a meeting had taken place was not in question, but the date was; Hua had been in Chengdu, Sichuan, on June 3.

2. In the second of the three instructions Mao gave Hua (April 30), Jiang Qing substituted "Act according to the principles laid down" for "Act according to past principles." The significance of this change was obvious: if Mao had asked Politburo to help his wife carry on the Red Banner, then this was the principle laid down, and Jiang Qing was the intended successor.

The news media, under Jiang's control, now played up the chairman's "deathbed adjuration"; and on September 16 the *Renmin Ribao* [People's daily], *Hongqi* [Red flag], and the *Liberation Army Daily* jointly editorialized, "Chairman Mao Will Live Forever in Our Hearts," stressing Mao's behest to "act according to the principles laid down." Hua was enraged, taking note of the three Chinese characters that had been altered from the original version. Hua believed the succession should be decided according to past principles; the first vice-chairman of the party should logically succeed the deceased chairman until the next plenary session of the Central Committee elected a new chairman.

At the memorial service on September 18, Hua retaliated in a masterly veiled speech in which he quoted Mao's famous dictum, "Political power grows out of the barrel of a gun," implying that he had the support of the military. Hua also quoted Mao's command, the "Three do's and don't's": (1) "Practice Marxism and not revisionism"; (2) "Unite, don't split"; and (3) "Be open and aboveboard, and don't intrigue and conspire."[18] The significance of this quotation could not be lost, for on the occasion of the original command, Mao had warned his wife and her cohorts "not to function as a gang of four." Hua still made no mention of the third instruction Mao gave him.

While Hua's speech could possibly have revealed too much of his intentions for his own good, in the confusion of the moment his opponents appeared to have taken no particular notice. To prevent any suspicion he allowed the Gang to continue to play important roles in state affairs.[19] The Gang continued to believe that it was both safe and strong.

The October 6 Coup

Several stormy Politburo meetings took place toward the end of September. On or about the 29th Hua pointed out the "wrong propaganda policy" of emphasizing the deathbed adjuration and neglecting the "Three do's and don't's." Jiang Qing responded that Hua was incompetent to lead the party and demanded that she be made chairman of the Central Committee. Hua retorted that he was not only competent but knew how to "solve problems"—in retrospect an ominous reference to his intention to remove the Four. The meeting ended inconclusively. On September 30 another meeting was called to discuss the National Day Ceremonies on October 1. On that occasion Hua led the procession of the Politburo members for picture taking. The photos (under Yao's direction) showed Hua at the far left and Jiang in the center of the picture to extol her importance. Little did she know that this was to be her last public appearance.

The struggle escalated in the early days of October. The "deathbed adjuration" appeared forty-two times in the *Renmin Ribao* [People's daily] and the *Guangming Daily*, compared with eleven times for the "Three do's and don't's." The Gang, still oblivious to the impending doom, was preparing to celebrate their ultimate victory. Jiang Qing and Wang Hongwen had numerous portraits taken in anticipation of the "top happy news."[20]

The Gang secretly set October 6 as the date of their coup. On October 2 they asked Mao Yuanxin to dispatch an armored division from Mukden (Shenyang) to Beijing, and the deputy chief-of-staff to transfer the 21st regimen from Baozhe, Shaanxi, to the capital. The Gang planned to set up a headquarters with Wang Dongxing and his 8341 special unit as the chief instrument of their coup, but the plan underwent a last-minute change as the Gang developed doubts about Wang's loyalty. They decided instead to rely on the 38th regiment stationed in Beijing.

October 4 was a momentous day. A bold article by Liang Xiao in the *Guangming Daily* stated that Mao's adjuration would "forever be the guide for continuous advance and the guarantee of victory to the members of the Chinese Communist Party. . . . All chieftains of the revisionist line who attempt to tamper with this principle laid down necessarily have to tamper with Marxist-Leninist-Mao Zedong Thought." "Past chieftains" were specifically named: Liu Shaoqi, Lin Biao, Chen Boda, and Deng Xiaoping. It warned that no revisionist chieftain would dare to challenge Mao's adjuration, meaning, of course, Hua. The anti-Gang forces regarded this article as a "mobilization order" and were ready to strike.[21]

In the early morning of October 5, a secret meeting was held in the headquarters of the commander of the People's Liberation Army, with five participants: Hua, Ye, Wang, Beijing Garrison Commander Chen Xilian, and Vice-Premier Li Xiannian (an ally of Deng Xiaoping). They decided to act decisively and quickly before the Gang could stage their coup by arresting all four leaders in a single swoop. Hua and Ye assumed overall direction with Chen Xilian assigned the duty of safeguarding Beijing and Wang Dongxing, the job of arresting the Four. Hua dispatched soldiers to guard the Great Wall against possible attack from Mukden and transferred another regiment to Beijing to watch over the 38th regiment. Meanwhile, the Guangzhou Military Region was alerted to ready two divisions for airlift to Beijing on instant notice.

Hua next invited the Four to attend an emergency Politburo meeting at midnight, October 5, at the party headquarters in Zhongnanhai. Wang Hongwen arrived first. He resisted arrest and killed two guards but was himself wounded and subdued. Then came Zhang Chunqiao and Yao Wenyuan; both fell into the trap. Jiang Qing was in bed when her captors arrived. She shouted: "How dare you to rebel when the Chairman's body is not yet cold!"[22] Others arrested included Mao Yuanxin, Minister of Culture Yu Huiyong, and Nanjing Military Region Commander Ding Sheng. In the small hours of October 6, the Gang was felled in one clean sweep. The Four were placed in solitary confinement in separate locations in Beijing.

On October 7 Hua Guofeng and Wang Dongxing each delivered two reports and Ye Jianying, one, to the Politburo. These reports, containing detailed charges against the Four, must have been prepared in extreme secrecy some time prior to the arrest. The Gang had been so smoothly and resolutely smashed that no question of civil strife arose; the success must be credited to the three protagonists who had long years of experience in security and military matters. The grateful Politburo named Hua chairman of the party Central Committee and concurrently chairman of the Military Commission, and put him in charge of editing the fifth volume of the *Selected Works of Mao Zedong*.[23]

Strictly speaking, the process of the selection of Hua as Mao's successor was of dubious legality. Article 9 of the party constitution stimulated that the party chairman must be elected in a plenary session of the Central Committee, and the Third Plenary Session of the Tenth Central Committee had not yet met. But the party and the country were willing to overlook

Hua Guofeng, immediate successor to Mao as party chairman (and premier).

the legal formality and make Hua the new leader at once. Much publicity was now given to Mao's message to Hua, "With you in charge, I am at ease," to create the image that Hua was the "anointed" successor.

On October 24 a million soldiers and civilians held a victory rally at Tian An Men Square to celebrate the smashing of the Gang of Four. A smiling Hua appeared, accompanied by top military leaders indicating the key role the military had played in the "palace revolution" and its continued support of Hua. Hua was hailed as a "worthy leader" of the party, a "worthy helmsman" to succeed Mao, and a brilliant leader who most nearly possessed the merits of Mao and Zhou.[24] The following day, the *Renmin Ribao* [People's daily], *Hongqi* [Red flag], and the *Liberation Army Daily*, under new management, jointly editorialized a "Great Historic Victory." Later, the Third Plenary Session of the Tenth Central Committee (July 1977) described the smashing of the Gang of Four as the eleventh major struggle in the history of the party, of almost equal importance with the Zunyi Conference (1935) and credited Hua with saving the revolution and the party.[25]

Several factors accounted for Hua's success. As first vice-chairman of the party and premier of the State Council, he had all the advantages of an incumbent leader. He enjoyed the support of the military and party leaders, and had won the cooperation of Wang Dongxing and the 8341 unit. He had taken the pulse of the country and knew the people's hatred of Jiang Qing and the Gang; in smashing them he was expressing the "common aspiration" of the people. And finally, having been a member of the committee investigating the Lin Biao affair, he knew that indecision was the chief cause of Lin's downfall and therefore acted decisively and swiftly to surprise and overwhelm the conspirators.

On the other hand, the Gang's failure must be traced first and foremost to the death of Mao. Under Mao's patronage the Four issued orders in his name and rode roughshod over the uncooperative. They mistreated thousands of respected elders and leaders, and used terrorists and secret agents to browbeat unsympathetic intellectuals and the people. In addition, the Gang led decadent, privileged, bourgeois private lives. Jiang Qing, for example, kept a "silver" jet for her own use, enjoyed the most expensive of German photographic equipment, wore silk blouses, and received guests in lavish settings.[26] While these excesses alienated the masses and mocked the ideals of the Chinese revolution, Mao's patronage of the Gang effectively stilled criticism.

The second major source of the Gang's weakness was the imbalance between military strength and media control. The Gang did not control the army but only the militia, which lacked organization and firepower, so they relied heavily on their control of the media and cultural scene to mold public opinion and to give an exaggerated image of power. Perhaps the loud support and broad coverage they received lured them into believing that they were stronger than they actually were. Moreover, Jiang Qing was overly confident that as Mao's wife, nobody would dare oppose her. But the fact was, the minute she became his widow, her fate was sealed.

Charges Against the Gang

On December 10, 1976, the Central Committee issued a 118-page document in four parts, *Zhongfa* 24, entitled "Evidence of Crime of the Anti-Party Clique of Wang Hongwen, Zhang Chungiao, Jiang Qing and Yao Wenyuan." Part I deals with the Gang's attempted "usurpation of the Party and seizure of power." Evidence includes the report of a secret visit by Wang to Mao in October 1974 accusing the hospitalized Zhou of conspiring with Deng, Ye, and others. Wang hoped to arouse Mao's suspicion and have Zhou dismissed. Another piece of evidence was the testimony of Mao's niece Wang Hairong that Jiang Qing aspired to be chairman, with Wang Hongwen and Zhang Chunqiao in top government positions.

Part II deals with the Gang's crime of adulterating the line laid down by Mao. In a February article, "On the Correct Handling of Contradictions Among the People," Mao pointed out that revisionism and rightist opportunism were more dangerous than dogmatism, and during his tour of the country in 1971 Mao announced the basic principles which became the "Three do's and don't's." The Gang did not follow Mao's line but overtly adulterated it by stressing empiricism as the most immediate danger.

Part III deals with alleged crimes against Hua Guofeng after he became acting premier (February 7, 1976) and premier-first-vice-chairman (April 7). The Gang was charged with adulterating Mao's instructions to Hua ("Act according to past principles") by prompting Liang Xiao to disseminate a fabricated version to news media and by opposing the Central Committee headed by Hua. Part IV concerns the Gang's attack on the party during Mao's illness and after his death.[27]

The Four were permanently expelled from the party, removed from all official posts, and branded as conspirators, ultrarightists, counterrevolutionaries, and representatives of Kuomintang.

From the Western standpoint, neither political machination nor aspiration to the highest offices in a country is a crime, but to conspire to overthrow the government is. The evidence against the Gang may be insufficient to substantiate the charges. What was clearly criminal was the Gang's unauthorized issuance of orders in the name of Mao, their killing of hundreds of thousands through their agents, their intimidation of people through terrorism and torture, and their disruption of education and industrial production, setting the country back by decades. Yet does not the ultimate responsibility for all this rest with Mao?

MAO AND THE GANG

There is no way to dissociate Mao from the Gang. Without him there could have been no Gang, for without his wife they would have had no safely protected leader. Jiang Qing, a former left-wing movie actress, came to Yenan after the Long March and became Mao's secretary. They fell in love and Mao asked for her hand, much to the consternation of Mao's third wife who protested violently and refused to divorce him. Senior cadres also disapproved of the marriage, but nonetheless the two were married in 1939. Reportedly, before the marriage senior officials exacted a promise from Mao that his wife not be active in politics for life or at least twenty years.[28]

It was only after the establishment of the People's Republic that Jiang received a minor appointment from Premier Zhou as a member of the Film Steering Committee in 1950. She was a delegate to the Third National People's Congress in 1954. Apart from these minor involvements, she lived a quiet life in poor health until 1958.

However, as her health improved in the early 1960s, the twenty-year waiting period had come to an end, and she became more active. In 1962 she reviewed for Mao the Peking Opera's repertoire and recommended that many works be banned. At this time she was introduced to Zhang Chunqiao, chief of the propaganda department in Shanghai, and writer Yao Wenyuan. With their help Jiang Qing carried out the reform of the Peking opera and offered several model revolutionary plays including *The Red Lantern* and *Taking Tiger Mountain by Strategy*. This won Mao's approval, and Jiang Qing gradually became his spokesman in art, literature, and culture. In 1965 Mao and Jiang directed Yao to write the essay entitled "Comment on the New Historical Play *Hai Rui Dismissed from Office*," which became the opening shot of the Cultural Revolution. In 1966, a Central Cultural Revolutionary Committee was formed with Chen Boda (Mao's secretary) as chairman, and Jiang Qing as first vice-chairman, a position of national prominence. The original Cultural Revolutionary Group thus consisted of Mao, Jiang Qing, Zhang Chunqiao Yao Wenyuan, and Chen Boda.

Mao had said: "Revolution hinges on the barrel of the gun and on the pen." In his struggle with Liu Shaoqi, Mao relied on the pens of the Jiang Qing group to dominate the propaganda machine, and the guns of Lin Biao to provide security and military support. Lin became a close ally of Mao and to ingratiate himself with Jiang Qing, asked her to preside over the army's Literary and Art Work Forum and appointed her advisor to the army's Cultural Revolutionary Group. Thus in the second stage of the development of the Cultural Revolutionary Group, Lin was an ally of Jiang Qing.

After the successive fiascos of naming first Liu and then Lin as his successors, Mao seemed frustrated and discouraged at the thought of naming yet another. He felt he could trust no one except his own assertive wife to carry on his ideas of revolution. So step by step he arranged for her to advance to the forefront of national politics. In his 1973 New Year Message, Mao declared: "The trade unions, the Communist Youth League, the Red Guard, the Little Red Soldiers, poor and lower-middle peasants and women's organizations should be consolidated step by step." Thus in one stroke the Cultural Revolutionary Group gained control of mass organizations, especially the trade union federations.

Next, Mao's plan involved increasing the Group's prominence at the Tenth Party Congress in August 1973. The Group now included Wang Hongwen, the fiery Shanghai cotton-mill worker who organized workers and masses to topple the

Shanghai mayor and party secretary. Wang was catapulted to a vice-chairmanship of the party, with Zhang Chunqiao on the Standing Committee of the Politburo, and Jiang Qing and Yao Wenyuan both Politburo members. In all, the Cultural Revolutionaries accounted for three of the five vice-chairmen of the party, four of the nine members of the Politburo Standing Committee, and eleven of the twenty-one members of the Politburo. They were clearly placed in strategic positions poised for the ultimate assumption of supreme power.

Mao's third strategy was to create large-scale militia units to rival the People's Liberation Army, with Wang Hongwen in charge of the model Shanghai militia. Wang was also made a vice-chairman of the influential Military Commission, while Zhang Chunqiao became director of the General Political Department of the People's Liberation Army, infiltrating the regular military establishment.

Jiang Qing's position received a further boost during Premier Zhou's illness when she received foreign visitors in her capacity as a state leader. Between May and October, 1974, she had received Archbishop Makarios, President Gnassingbe Eyadema of Togo, the head of the Nigerian Federal Military Government, and others, although by November she stopped receiving state visitors, perhaps due to the criticism of party seniors. Meanwhile party writers circulated inspiring stories about Empress Lü (187–179 B.C.) and female-emperor Wu Zetian (A.D. 684–705), implying that Jiang Qing, too, could be a good ruler.

As Zhou's condition worsened, it appeared that Deng Xiaoping would assume control of the State Council as premier. But in the fall of 1975 Mao launched an "Antirightist Deviationist" Campaign against Deng, and after Zhou's death, Deng disappeared from public view. Mao then chose Hua Guofeng to be acting premier and later premier and first vice-chairman of the party in April 1976 primarily to stop Deng from returning to power. It is likely Mao hoped that Hua, who had gained prominence during the Cultural Revolution, would be a transitional figure who would assist Jiang Qing to power. But, as the old Chinese saying goes, "A wise man may calculate a thousand times, but inevitably there will be a miss!"

Mao realized his wife's "wide ambitions" to become chairman, and he also knew of the countless number of people she had wronged, harmed, arrested, or killed during the decade of the Cultural Revolution. On July 17, 1974, Mao had warned the Gang: "You'd better be careful; don't let yourselves become a small faction of four." In May 1975 he admonished them with the "Three do's and don't's," ending with, "Don't function as a gang of four; don't do it anymore."[29] Mao was thus aware of the Gang's excesses and could have restrained their leader by a simple order. That this was not done reflected his failings as party chairman and the Great Helmsman.

When the American playwright Arthur Miller visited China in 1978, he met with Chinese writers, artists, movie directors, and stage managers. He learned that many of the country's leading artists and intellectuals had been killed or imprisoned and tortured. To Miller it was inconceivable that Jiang alone could have committed such injustices without the support of Mao. Quoting Mao, "People are no chives; their heads do not grow back when they are cut off," Miller concluded: "It has become impossible to believe that a 'faction' could have swung the People's Republic around its head without the consent of the Great Helmsman."[30] For Miller, Mao's lack of leadership could not be blamed on his physical infirmity, for people were jailed and killed in the 1960s when he was still strong enough to swim six and one-half kilometers in the Yangtze River. Miller's final judgment: the Gang of Four was "merely a screen for the still-sacrosanct name of Mao."[31]

Although deified before 900 million people, Mao in private life was an aged and doddering husband. As he increasingly submitted to Jiang Qing's pressure, he lost all sense of proportion in state affairs. A communism tinted with familial favoritism smacks of "socialist feudalism." Yet from the dramatic events of 1976, the defeat of extremism, and indeed of lawlessness, there came a promise of greater stability, better life, and a new drive for modernization.

NOTES

1. *The New York Times,* Jan. 9, 1976, pp. 11–12.
2. Ch'en Yung-sheng, "The 'October 6th Coup' and Hua Kuo-feng's Rise to Power," *Issues & Studies,* XV:10:81–82 (Oct. 1979).
3. Mao had likened himself to this first emperor of the Qin dynasty who unified China in 221 B.C.
4. Text of Central Committee announcement in English carried by *The New York Times,* April 8, 1976, p. 16.
5. *Peking Review,* Dec. 24, 1976, p. 8. See also Richard C. Thorton, "The Political Succession to Mao Tse-tung," *Issues & Stuides,* XIV:6:35 (June 1978).
6. There were 240,000 dead and 164,000 injured. *Los Angeles Times,* June 11, 1977.
7. Julie Nixon Eisenhower.
8. *The Times,* London, Sept. 10, 1976, p. 7; *International Herald Tribune,* Paris, Sept. 10, 1976, pp. 1, 3.
9. Chien T'ieh, "The Chiang Ch'ing Faction and People's Military Forces," *Issues & Studies,* XII:1:23 (Jan. 1976).
10. *Peking Review,* Feb. 4, 1977, pp. 5–10; Andres D. Onate, "Hua Kuo-feng and the Arrest of the 'Gang of Four'," *The China Quarterly,* 75:555–56 (Sept. 1978).
11. Onate, p. 555.
12. *Ibid.,* pp. 558–89.
13. Zhu De (1886–1976) died in July 1976 of undisclosed causes, and his son-in-law, General Pi Dingzhun, was killed in a mysterious airplane crash en route to Zhu's funeral.
14. Ch'en Yung-sheng, p. 78.
15. Testimony by Zhang Binghua, former director of the Propaganda Department of the CCP Central Committee, quoted in Ch'en Yung-sheng, pp. 85–86.
16. Onate, p. 556.
17. *Ibid.,* p. 549.
18. Complete text of the speech in *Peking Review,* Sept. 24, 1976, pp. 12–16.
19. On September 26, 1976, Zhang Chunqiao signed an international trade and economic agreement with Jamaica, and on September 30 the Gang of Four joined other leaders in a forum atop the Tian An Men.
20. *People's Daily,* Dec. 17, 1976; Onate, pp. 552–53.
21. *People's Daily,* Dec. 17, 1976.
22. Reported in *Central Daily News,* Taipei, Sept. 23, 1980.
23. The selection of Hua, although supposedly made on October 7,

was possibly made later. In the initial Politburo announcement of October 7, there was no mention of Hua's appointment. The October 29, 1976, issue of *Peking Review* carried an article, "Great Historic Victory" (p. 14) which belatedly stated: "In accordance with the arrangements Chairman Mao had made before he passed away, the October 7, 1976 resolution of the Central Committee of the Communist Party appointed Comrade Hua Guofeng chairman of the Central Committee of the Communist Party of China and Chairman of the Military Commission of the C.P.C. Central Committee."

24. "Comrade Hua Kuo-feng Is Our Party's Worthy Leader" and "Great Historic Victory," both in *Peking Review*, No. 44, Oct. 29, 1976, pp. 14–16; No. 45, Nov. 5, 1976, pp. 5–6.
25. *Peking Review*, No. 47, Nov. 19, 1976.
26. Roxane Witke, *Comrade Chiang Ch'ing* (Boston, 1977), pp. 37–38.
27. Complete text of the charges in *Issues and Studies*, Sept., Oct., 1977.
28. Witke, pp. 148–57, 335.
29. Joint editorials of *Renmin Ribao* [People's daily], *Hongqi* [Red flag], and *Liberation Army Daily*, Oct. 25, 1976.
30. Inge Morath and Arthur Miller, *Chinese Encounters* (New York, 1979), pp. 21, 40.
31. *Ibid.*, p. 7.

FURTHER READING

Chang, Chen-pang, "Mao Tse-tung and the Gang of Four," *Issues & Studies*, XIII:9:18–33 (Sept. 1977).

Ch'en, Yung-sheng, "The 'October 6th Coup' and Hua Kuo-feng's Rise to Power," *Issue & Studies*, XV:10:75–86 (Oct. 1979).

Cheng, J. Chester, *Documents of Dissent: Chinese Political Thought Since Mao* (Stanford, 1981).

Chi, Hsin, *The Rise and Fall of the "Gang of Four"* (tr. from *The Seventies Magazine*), (New York, 1977).

Domes, Jürgen, "The Gang of Four and Hua Fuo-feng: An Analysis of Political Events in 1975–76," *The China Quarterly*, 71: 473–97 (Sept. 1977).

Fox, Galen, "Campaigning for Power in China," *Contemporary China*, III:1:80–95 (Spring 1979).

"Great Historic Victory," *Peking Review*, 44:14–16 (Oct. 29, 1976).

"How the 'Gang of Four' Used Shanghai as a Base to Usurp Party and State Power," *Peking Review*, 6:5–10 (Feb. 4, 1977).

Hsü, Kai-yu, *The Chinese Literary Scene: A Writer's Visit to the People's Republic* (New York, 1975).

Liu, Alan P. L., "The Gang of Four and the Chinese People's Liberation Army," *Asian Survey*, XIX:9:817–37 (Sept. 1979).

"Mao Tse-tung (1893–1976)—the Man Who Changed the Life of China," *International Herald Tribune*, Paris, Sept. 10, 1976.

"Mao Tse-tung," *The Times*, London, Sept. 10, 1976.

Morath, Inge, and Arthur Miller, *Chinese Encounters* (New York, 1979).

Nee, Victor, and James Peck (eds.), *China's Uninterrupted Revolution* (New York, 1975).

Oksenberg, Michel, and Sai-cheung Yeung, "Hua Kuo-feng's Pre-Cultural Revolution Hunan Years, 1946–66: The Making of a Political Generalist," *The China Quarterly*, 69:3–53 (March 1977).

Oksenberg, Michel, "Evaluating the Chinese Political System," *Contemporary China*, III:2:102–111 (Summer 1979).

Onate, Andres D., "Hua Kuo-feng and the Arrest of the 'Gang of Four,'" *The China Quarterly*, 75:540–65 (Sept. 1978).

Roots, John McCook, *An Informal Biography of China's Legendary Chou En-lai* (New York, 1978).

"Tough New Man in Peking," *Time* Magazine, Jan. 19, 1976, pp. 24–31.

Tsou, Tang, "Mao Tse-tung Thought, the Last Struggle for Succession, and the Post-Mao Era," *The China Quarterly*, 71:498–527 (Sept. 1977).

Uhalley, Stephen, Jr., *Mao Tse-tung: A Critical Biography* (New York, 1975).

Wang, Hsueh-wen, "The 'Gang of Four' Incident: Official Exposé by a CCPCC Document," *Issues & Studies*, XIII:9:46–58 (Sept. 1977).

Wei, Hua, and Tang Hsiao, "A Criticism of Chang Chun-chiao's 'Thoughts on February 3, 1976,'" *Peking Review*, 5:16–18 (Jan. 28, 1977).

Wilson, Dick (ed.), *Mao Tse-tung in the Scales of History: A Preliminary Assessment Organized by the China Quarterly* (Cambridge, Eng., 1977).

Witke, Roxane, *Comrade Chiang Ch'ing* (Boston, 1977).

Wong, Paul, *China's Higher Leadership in the Socialist Transition* (New York, 1976).

2

Deng Xiaoping
and China's New Order

Since the cataclysmic year 1976, the changes wrought by the party, the government, and the people of China have altered the surface as well as the depths of Chinese politics. Beginning with Deng Xiaoping's quick return to power, China's priorities were thoroughly reorganized. In the meetings of party and government councils, in the communications media, and in the actions of the average citizen a cry for change was heard: for normalcy, stability, and most notably, for modernization and the material and cultural benefits it implied. By analyzing the proceedings of the party and government meetings, examining the assertions of the media, and paying special attention to private manipulations as well as to the expressions of the common people, a reasonably accurate picture of China's "new beginning" can be drawn.

Following the downfall of the Gang of Four, Chairman Hua Guofeng faced three pressing issues: (1) his legitimacy as Mao's successor; (2) the rehabilitation of Deng Xiaoping; and (3) the reordering of economic priorities to promote modernization. Regarding the succession, Mao's instruction to Hua ("With you in charge, I am at ease") was regarded by Ye and

Deng supporters[1] as reflecting Mao's personal view rather than the will of the party, whose constitution has specific provisions governing the election of the party chairman. By implication, Hua's assumption of the chairmanship of the Central Committee and of its Military Commission was deemed unconstitutional; but, if he would agree to the reinstatement of Deng, this question of legitimacy could be negotiated or even withdrawn. Thus, the two issues came into balance. As a result of mediation by Marshal Ye and Vice-Premier Li Xiannian, who desperately desired a smooth transition to the post-Mao era, Hua agreed in principle to rehabilitate Deng, and to revise the five-year economic plan to accelerate the Four Modernizations. In late November 1976 Hua announced that Deng's reinstatement would be discussed at the next Central Committee meetings in July 1977. In return, he received support from Ye, Li, and others for chairmanship of the Central Committee and its Military Commission.

DENG'S REHABILITATION

Deng's many supporters in the party and the army had mounted an extensive campaign demanding his rehabilitation. At the first anniversary of Zhou Enlai's death in January 1977, there were demonstrations and wall posters in Beijing calling for Deng's return to office. The Politburo which met that month cleared Deng of involvement in the Tian An Men Square Incident of April 1976, reclassifying his case from "antagonistic contradiction" to "contradiction among the people," i.e. rectifiable. Hua polled the 200-odd Central Committee members as to their views on the Deng case, and in March the Politburo agreed to restore Deng to all his former positions, provided he admit his past mistakes.

Deng wrote two letters to Hua, Ye, and the Central Committee, and in the second he said: "I firmly welcome Mr. Hua as chairman of our party. I firmly support the crushing of the Gang of Four by the party Central Committee under

Chairman Hua. I am well and I ask Chairman Hua to send me to the front line [of work]."[2] Hua replied: "You have made mistakes and you should be criticized. [But] you are not responsible for the Tian An Men Square Incident. Not only will you be sent to the front line, but to the firing line [of work]."[3] In May Deng's two letters were distributed by Hua to cadres at different levels and they won the approval "of all comrades in the party."[4] Meanwhile, in volume five of the *Selected Works of Mao Zedong* edited by Hua and released in April 1977, there appeared no less than nine passages praising Deng's political stance in the 1950s.

While negotiating Deng's rehabilitation, Hua also labored to refine his image as an advocate of modernization and as an expert in economics. He attended a number of conferences on agriculture, finance, banking, and industry including the national conference on agriculture at Dazhai in December 1976 and the industrial conference at Daqing in April and May 1977. At the same time, Hua, Ye, and Deng all intensified their efforts to appoint provincial party secretaries in an attempt to strengthen their respective positions at the next two vital party meetings: the Third Plenum of the Tenth Central Committee and the Eleventh Party Congress in July and August 1977. Their maneuvers resulted in the appointment of four Hua supporters,[5] four Ye supporters,[6] and five Deng supporters[7] in addition to Zhao Ziyang, party first secretary of Sichuan since December 1975.

In the Third Plenum of the Tenth Central Committee meeting, three resolutions were passed to confirm earlier Politburo decisions. First was the approval of Hua as chairman of the party and of the Military Commission; next was the acceptance of Hua's recommendation that Deng be restored to his former posts—Politburo Standing Committee member, vice-chairman of the Central Committee, first deputy premier of the State Council, vice-chairman of the Military Commission, and chief of the General Staff of the Liberation Army—all top positions in the military, the party, and the government. The third resolution condemned the antiparty activities of the Gang of Four and accused them of "conspiring to overthrow Comrade Zhou Enlai," of "violently attacking and falsely accusing Comrade Deng Xiaoping," of being "extremely hostile and thoroughly opposed to" Mao's choice of Hua, and of "plotting to overthrow the party Central Committee headed by Comrade Hua Guofeng and bring about a counterrevolutionary restoration." The Four were officially expelled from the party for good.[8]

With the Gang of Four and their chief supporters removed, the party began a vast personnel reshuffle. The party approved the appointments of Mao's former bodyguard Wang Dongxing and Vice-Premier Li Xiannian to the Politburo Standing Committee, boosting the membership to nine. At the close of the Tenth Central Committee meetings, Hua's supporters slightly outnumbered Deng's, with Ye's providing a balance between them. It is of note that in the Central Committee itself, 84 percent of the 201 members were veteran party cadres and military leaders, a third of whom had been victims of the Cultural Revolution and now filled the seats vacated by Gang supporters.

The Eleventh Party Congress held between August 12–18, 1977, continued the personnel reshuffle. Hua retained the party chairmanship, and four vice-chairmen were appointed: Ye, Deng, Li Xiannian, and Wang Dongxing. These five constituted the Standing Committee of the Politburo. The Politburo itself had ten new faces, and its power structure fell roughly into the following three groups: Hua and Deng each had nine supporters and Ye five.[9] With none of the three in command of a majority, Ye continued to hold the balance. Yet certain changes, such as Hua's relinquishment of the post of minister of public security to a Deng supporter (Zhao Cangbi), indicated Deng's growing power.

In spite of the emerging power struggles, the Congress closed with a call for unity, discipline, stability, and cooperation—a sharp contrast to the continuous upheaval and factional strife that characterized the Mao era. A Disciplinary Committee was established to monitor the conduct of 35 million party members. In many ways the Congress seemed to signal the beginning of the end of the Maoist era.

DENG'S DRIVE FOR POLITICAL DOMINANCE

Personnel changes made in the party meetings discussed above must not be confused with government appointments. Government appointments recommended by the party must be approved by the National People's Congress. Hence, the Fifth People's Congress was scheduled for the spring of 1978, and to prepare for its convocation it was decided that all twenty-nine provincial revolutionary committee leaders had to be re-elected. By February 1978 the re-election process had been completed and the Congress convened accordingly from February 26 to March 5, 1978.

Enlargement of the Power Base

A key issue at the Congress was whether or not the post of the state chairmanship, occupied previously by Mao and Liu Shaoqi, should be resurrected; it was decided in the negative. Ye accepted the chairmanship of the Congress's Standing Committee, a sort of titular headship of state formerly occupied by Zhu De until his death in 1976. There was much talk about Deng's advancement to the premiership, but Hua retained the position. Deng consolidated his power as first deputy premier in charge of the Four Modernizations. Fang Yi, a protegé of both Ye and Deng, was made responsible for the development of science and technology, the basis of the other modernizations (agriculture, industry, and national defense). Another important post, the chairmanship of the State Planning Commission, went to Yu Qiuli, a veteran economic planner and Deng supporter. Such appointments demonstrated the give-and-take among the leaders in hopes of achieving some semblance of equilibrium.

At the close of the Congress, Hua called for unity, modernization, better international relations, a 10 percent industrial growth, and a 4 to 5 percent annual increase in agricultural expansion. These targets seemed overly ambitious, in some cases more than doubling recent average increases. However,

Military statesman Marshal Ye Jianying.

in the euphoric atmosphere of the post-Gang period, ambition and progress were the order of the day; nothing seemed impossible, however unrealistic to the critical eye.

At the same time, in spite of the unity represented by the three-way coalition of Hua, Ye, and Deng, tension continued to mount. On the surface, Hua and Deng maintained a working relationship; Hua treated Deng with due respect as a party senior of the Long March generation, while Deng treated Hua with the courteous condescension that an elder Chinese family member exhibits toward a younger one. Yet Deng's strategy for political domination put him in conflict with Hua. Deng's growing power as well as his strategy were obvious enough, but Hua lacked the organization to halt it.

Deng was intent upon enlarging his power base by rehabilitating men who had suffered under Mao and the Gang in the name of "righting the wrong" (*pingfan*). He took a strong stand against leaders associated with the Cultural Revolution and the Gang of Four, especially those who had criticized him and blocked his succession to Zhou Enlai. These included

Hua (who rose under Mao's patronage), Wang Dongxing (head of Mao's bodyguard), Wu De (mayor of Beijing), and Ji Dengkui (a doctrinaire Politburo member). Deng attacked not Hua but his associates, chiselling away at his political periphery so that the center would be rendered hollow. Meanwhile, Deng also cultivated able, younger followers, placing them in key positions so that they could perpetuate his economic policies.

Deng, however, did not limit himself to attacks on individuals or the appointments of "young blood"; he simultaneously eroded the ideological power base of his former adversaries by combatting the embedded supremacy of "Mao Thought." To this he announced in May and June of 1978 two clever guiding principles: "Practice is the sole criterion of truth" and "Seek truth from facts." By implication Mao Zedong's thought was no longer the standard by which a policy or an action must be judged; in fact, the thought itself must be subject to the scrutiny of facts, practice, and truth. The problem of Mao's leadership and his responsibility for the Cultural Revolution and China's ills became a major concern of the post-Gang government.

The Fifth National People's Congress met again from June 18 to July 1, 1979, to deliberate and ratify earlier decisions reached by the party Central Committee in December 1978. The ratifications involved: (1) establishing the primacy of agriculture and of speeding its development; (2) shifting the focus of state and party work to socialist construction while revising overly ambitious targets for the Four Modernizations; (3) enacting a legal system for the protection and enhancement of democracy; and (4) approving key personnel changes in government.

The parliamentlike Congress had a presidium chaired by the elder statesman Ye with the help of Secretary General Ulanfu, an ethnic minority leader and Deng supporter. The Dengists clearly dominated the day. Peng Zhen, former mayor of Beijing, disgraced during the Cultural Revolution, headed the Committee on Legal Code; Hu Yaobang, a Politburo member and head of party propaganda, directed the Committee on

The Democracy Wall in Beijing, 1979.

Qualifications of New Congress Delegates. Three new vice-premiers were appointed, all formerly victims of the Cultural Revolution: Chen Yun, Bo Ibo (both veteran economic planners), and Yao Yilin (formerly minister of commerce). The presidency of the Chinese Academy of Sciences went to Fang Yi. Deng was said to have declined the premiership, preferring the less assuming title of first deputy premier while exercising the de facto power of premier. Clearly, titles mean little in contemporary China; it is the exercise of power and the ability to control decisions that count.

Hua and Deng had apparently reached a tacit understanding; the former would support Deng's personnel changes and economic policies, while the latter would slow moves toward a critical assessment of Mao's role in the Cultural Revolution, which could prove both embarrassing and injurious to Hua. Nonetheless, the Congress's repeated calls for stability, unity, modernization, a legal system, and democracy were a subtle repudiation of Mao's rule, which had been marked by ceaseless upheaval, factional strife, and poor economic planning.

Hua himself announced that "the root causes of unending

political turmoil and splits" had been eliminated and that stability and unity were the desires of the people. He called for an acceleration in the development of agriculture and light industry in the next three years, accompanied by a realistic revision of the timetable for the Four Modernizations. He encouraged a restrained hope for democracy, a legal system, and material incentives when he implied that modernization would not succeed unless the majority of the people believed that a large measure of democracy had been granted.

In establishing realistic goals for modernization, economic reports were delivered which revealed important statistics for the first time in twenty years, suggesting a "return to normalcy." Food production in 1978 was up 7.8 percent from 1977, and the forecast for 1979 was 2.4 percent higher. Crude oil production rose 11.1 percent over 1977, and the growth in 1979 was estimated at 1.9 percent. The 1979 budget totalled Ch$112 billion, of which 18 percent was allocated to the military. Agriculture received a notable increase in investment from 10.7 percent to 14 percent of the budget. To alleviate the hardships of the farmer, whose per capita annual income was only Ch$75 ($48) in 1978 compared with Ch$664 ($430) for the average urban worker, the government raised farm products purchase prices so that farm income would increase by Ch$10 ($6.6) per farmer, a small but not insignificant improvement.[10]

The prospect of an improving economy, more realistic modernization goals, and a better protected democracy generated the Congress's closing spirit of national unity and stability. The sensitive issue of personnel change was resolved by adding new officials without dismissing existing ones and by allowing Chairman Hua to retain his premiership. Hua also scored something of a victory by championing the cause of farmers and by his ardent support of the Four Modernizations.

The Congress, however, signaled a more definite victory for Deng in the development of his economic policy and in the enhancement of his power base. In spite of their political rivalry, the Hua-Deng leadership was, above all, committed to a policy of national reconstruction through economic development and modernization, and to a new stability built on the fruits of this new order. However, the accomplishment of these goals was still predicted upon the four fundamental principles: the dictatorship of the proletariat, party leadership, the socialist line, and Marxism-Leninism and the Thought of Mao. Thus, no one knew how long the new state of greater relaxation and freedom would last.

"Economics in Command": Removal of Opponents and Introduction of "New Blood"

The Fifth Plenum of the Eleventh Central Committee (February 23–29, 1980) marked the end of the transitional period from Mao's death to the meteoric rise of Deng as the most powerful figure in Chinese politics. The party rejected Mao's "politics in command" for Deng's "economics in command" hoping to turn China into an advanced nation by the year 2000. Any activity or person deemed unsympathetic to this course would be curtailed or removed. Thus, though divergent views were allowed, acts of dissidence such as posters on "Democracy Wall" attacking the government were not tolerated. The Four Freedoms—to speak out freely, to air one's views fully, to engage in great debates, and to write big-character posters— were deleted from the party constitution. Both the government and the party were fearful that the delicate stability might be disturbed by too large a dosage of unaccustomed freedom; yet they were determined not to stifle the creativity, initiative, and enthusiasm that the new national goals generated. Their compromise resulted in a "restrained democracy" with moderate controls.

The trend toward eliminating dissension was not limited to Democracy Wall. Four Politburo members who were lukewarm or unsympathetic toward Deng and his policy were relieved of their high party and government posts. Three of them were linked to the Cultural Revolution: Wang Dongxing (a party vice-chairman and formerly Mao's chief bodyguard), Wu De (former mayor of Beijing), and Ji Dengkui (vice-premier).

Deng Xiaoping, vice-chairman of the party and main architect of China's new order.

The fourth, General Chen Xilian, was formerly head of the Beijing Military Region.

On the other hand, two more of Deng's dynamic protégés were appointed to the Politburo Standing Committee—Zhao Ziyang, an effective party first secretary in Sichuan, and Hu Yaobang, Deng's right-hand man in party affairs. Hu also became head of the newly re-established party Secretariat in charge of the party's daily affairs. Four other Deng supporters were appointed to the Secretariat: Fang Yi (vice-premier and Academy of Sciences president), Yu Qiuli (vice-premier and head of the State Planning Commission), Peng Chong (veteran cadre), and Yang Deze (vice-minister of defense and chief of staff of the Armed Forces, a post now vacated by Deng).

Meanwhile, the rehabilitations that so benefited Deng continued. To clear the name of the former Chief of State Liu Shaoqi, who was disgraced and discredited along with Deng during the Cultural Revolution, the party resolved that he be posthumously restored to honor. On May 17, 1980, a national memorial service was held, and Liu was praised as a great

Hu Yaobang, new party chairman.

proletarian fighter. The occasion was viewed as a negation of the values of the Cultural Revolution and a denial of Mao's infallibility.

From the personnel changes it is apparent that the new party line was to introduce "new blood" at the highest level. To this end the party approved Deng's idea of a "collective leadership" capable of carrying on the party line irrespective of the fate of the present leaders.

Hua's Resignation from the Premiership

At the Third Plenum of the Fifth National People's Congress (August 29–September 10, 1980) the Dengists rose to the pinnacle of power. Deng had long urged separating party and government functions as well as ending lifelong appointments to cadres. The Congress approved his reorganization plan, insuring an orderly transfer of power to a collective leadership of relatively young pragmatists committed to modernization regardless of the fates of Deng and other aging leaders.

Hua graciously submitted his resignation as premier and nominated Zhao Ziyang as his successor. Deng and six other vice-premiers resigned for reasons of old age, other important appointments, or "voluntary" withdrawal. In the first category, apart from Deng, were Li Xiannian and Chen Yun, both seventy-five; Defense Minister Xu Xiangqian, seventy-eight; and Wang Zhen, a party military official, seventy-three. The second category included Wang Renzhong, who was also party minister of propaganda; and among those who withdrew "voluntarily" was Chen Yonggui, sixty-five, an illiterate model-peasant hand-picked by Mao and Zhou as the party's "token peasant" vice-premier.

As these resignations had been discussed in advance, their announcement aroused no surprise. What made news was the undiscussed appointment of three new vice-premiers: Foreign Minister Huang Hua, sixty-four; Minister of Nationality Affairs Yang Jingren, seventy-four; and General Zhang Aiping, seventy, the deputy army chief of staff. With these appointments, the total number of vice-premiers dropped from eighteen to fourteen. These new appointees were not particularly young and continued to hold their party positions. Five vice-chairmen of the People's Congress whose ages ranged from 79 to 88 resigned, but Ye, eighty-two, remained chairman of the Stand-

Premier Zhao Ziyang.

ing Committee of the Congress. Thus the principles of Deng's reorganization were not strictly followed. Hua's report on the personnel reshuffle, his last as premier, was warmly applauded by the 3,000 Congress delegates.

It should be noted that the National Congress was only concerned with government appointments. Those who retired or resigned did not lose their party positions. Hua remained chairman of the Central Committee and of its Military Commission; and Deng still held his party vice-chairmanship, and the four former vice-premiers, their seats on the Politburo. With Zhao as premier and Hu as party general secretary, the pragmatists were in firm control of both government and party. For the first time an orderly transfer of power was achieved while the previous incumbents were still healthy, creating a precedent for future leaders which might avoid the wrenching political turmoil and uncertainty of the past.

Deng believed the new system would perpetuate his policies of modernization while ridding the country of its tendency toward political cultism. In this regard, he had a broader perspective than Mao and was more successful in solving the succession problem. Mao's revolutionary romanticism now gave way to Deng's pragmatic nation-building in a new political order born of a new historical situation. Hua saw this and gracefully relinquished the premiership and his status as the sole successor to Mao. Further changes would surely unfold during the next party plenum in mid-1981.

With the emergence of a new order in the post-Mao era, China was to be run not by a single towering figure but by a group of pragmatic administrators with proven records of success. As former party first secretary in Sichuan (1975–80), Zhao Ziyang had achieved an economic miracle by lifting Sichuan from chaos to relative prosperity in four years— raising industrial output by 81 percent and grain output by 25 percent, and creating 600,000 new jobs. He encouraged private plots, sideline handicraft work, free markets, pay according to work, and greater autonomy for local industries. Zhao's executive vice-premier, Wan Li, formerly party first secretary in Anhui, had won fame for his farm modernization programs there. Zhao and Wan are expected to put their experience to work on a national scale, combining market forces with the planned economy of socialism. Zhao asserts that so long as the principles of public ownership of the means of production and pay according to work are maintained, any structure, system, policy, or measure that promotes production is acceptable. He said, "We must not bind ourselves as silk-worms do within cocoons. . . . All economic patterns which hold back development of production should be abolished." Such pragmatism reflects the new spirit of the government, anxious to make up for lost time.

THE DEMYSTIFICATION OF MAO

During the last fifteen years of his life, Mao, the Chinese "Lenin and Stalin combined," was sanctified as an all-knowing, all-wise demigod who could do no wrong. Millions waved the "Little Red Book" of quotations from Chairman Mao, chanting its passages like magic formulas that could turn defeat into victory. It was an incredible cult of personality that surpassed even Stalin's. The wonder was not so much that Mao permitted it, but that 900 million believed in it. Perhaps they really didn't, but for a time they surely acted as if they did.

Once Mao was dead and the Gang of Four smashed, Mao's image quickly became tarnished. His responsibility for the rise of the Gang was common knowledge; yet no one dared to debunk him as Khrushchev had Stalin. Leaders gingerly invoked Mao's sayings of the 1950s to refute his later policies, but deMaoification had to be handled with care because Hua, until the 1977 Party Congress had confirmed his status, derived the legitimacy of his position largely from Mao's patronage. Hua honored Mao's legacy in order to consolidate his own position while reinterpreting Mao to suit his need in the changing times and circumstances.

The foremost question facing the nation was how to deal with the question of Mao's responsibility for China's recent ills. Before any answers could be offered, the party had elevated Zhou Enlai to a position of near-parity with Mao, ending the solitary eminence of the Great Helmsman. Zhou's wife, Deng Yingchao, was appointed to a vice-chairmanship of the National People's Congress. That Mao's wife was in jail and Zhou's in high honor symbolized a national consensus reflecting the demystification of Mao.

The first year after Mao's death witnessed a growing sense

of relief and a movement toward a new beginning. The structural references introduced by Mao or the Gang apparently no longer fit the realities of life where stability, unity, discipline, and economic progress were the new order. The revolutionary rhetoric and cultural intolerance which had rendered China an intellectual desert of artistic insipidity gave way to some degree of relaxation and freedom of expression. The cultural straightjacket dictated by the Gang (e.g. that China needed only eight model operas, or "more knowledge means more reactionism") was now condemned as absurd and counterproductive. Beethoven, Mozart, and Shakespeare, once symbols of "bourgeois decadence and running dogs of imperialism," reappeared in mid-1977; so did the works of the great Tang poets Li Po and Tu Fu, "products of the feudal past." In September 1977, colleges and universities which had suffered frequent interruptions during the Cultural Revolution began to admit students through competitive entrance examinations based on academic performance rather than on political "redness," and the mandatory two-year rural apprenticeship was dropped. For the first time in a decade, China had a normal freshman class, which graduated in 1981.

In industry worker participation in management was no longer the first priority; professional personnel were installed wherever possible. To reward productivity, wages of workers were increased and material incentives used to boost work enthusiasm. The principle "from each according to his ability, to each according to his work" was adopted. State Planning Commission Chairman Yu Qiuli said: "We must combat the situation in which no one accepts responsibility. We must struggle against anarchism."[11] It was a direct slap at Mao's cultural revolutionary values.

With the rehabilitation of Deng in July 1977, Mao's desanctification was accelerated. First by indirect and later by open criticism, Mao's pedestal was chipped away. At the Eleventh Party Congress in August, Hua declared an end to the Cultural Revolution in contradiction of Mao's assertion that cultural revolution was a continuing process to be renewed every seven or eight years. Deng emphasized discipline and hard work to advance modernization: "There must be less empty talk and more hard work." The "empty talk" of the Cultural Revolution had offered no concrete improvements, and Deng's "economics in command" triumphed as the new line.

By mid-1978 Mao's demigod status was questioned in public. An article in a historical journal remarked that even the most farsighted and resourceful of historical figures should not be considered gods.[12] The *Renmin Ribao* [People's daily] chided some for treating Marxism-Leninism and the Thought of Mao as objects of faith rather than as knowledge: "They make this a blind faith and do not allow people to use their brains, much less to discern truth from falsehood. Marxism is a philosophy and not religious dogma."[13] Deng needed to loosen the country from the grip of Maoist strictures in order to launch his own program of rapid modernization, which was a revolution in itself, albeit of a different nature.

On July 1, 1978, the fifty-seventh anniversary of the founding of the Chinese Communist Party, a speech made by Mao in 1962 was reprinted to show that he confessed to mistakes and an ignorance of economic planning, industry, and commerce: "In socialist construction, we are still acting blindly to a very large degree. . . . I myself do not understand many problems in the work of economic construction . . . [or] much about industry and commerce. I understand something about agriculture but only relatively and a limited way. . . . When it comes to productive forces, I know very little."[14] The underlying message could not have been more clear—Mao was not an omniscient deity, but a fallible human being.

The second anniversary of Mao's death, September 9, 1978, passed without observance. Shortly after, the Red Guard, a symbol of Mao's support of the Cultural Revoltuion, was dissolved; both the "Little Red Book" and Mao's quotations on newspaper mastheads disappeared. On October 8 the "cult of Mao" was attacked in the *Renmin Ribao* [People's daily]: "The proletarian leaders are great but their greatness has a commonplace origin and it does not descend from heaven. To describe them as kinds of deities is to render to them the greatest insult. . . . For many years such superstition circumscribed the minds of some people, and they still need to have their minds emancipated."[15]

Throughout the second half of 1978 wall posters and articles continued to criticize Mao's mistakes, implying a concerted effort to demystify him and to erode his image as a god-hero. Increasingly the editorials of the *Renmin Ribao* [People's daily] referred to Mao as comrade rather than chairman, and criticisms of his role in the Cultural Revolution—now dubbed "Ten Years of Great Catastrophe"—became more pronounced. A Tianjin wall poster entitled "Spanking the Tiger's Hips" accused Mao of killing millions of people, of launching the Antirightist Movement (1957) which hurt hundreds of thousands of intellectuals, of prematurely creating communes (1958) thereby causing the starvation of millions, and of supporting the Gang of Four at the expense of senior cadres. A poster in Hangzhou decried Mao's involvement in the Korean War which drained scarce national resources, the Great Leap Forward which caused economic chaos and famine, and the Cultural Revolution which set the country back in every sphere.[16]

Deng's two principles, "Practice is the sole criterion of truth" and "Seek truth from facts," struck at the very heart of the Thought of Mao. Actually, verification of truth through practice is Marxist theory; and Mao's thought, until successfully practiced, could only be theory, not truth.[17] Mao himself had said: "We must believe in science and nothing else, that is to say, we must not be superstitious. . . . What is right is right and what is wrong is wrong—otherwise it is superstition."[18]

A poster displayed on November 22 in front of Tian An Men Square entitled "Five Questions" applied Deng's slogans to Mao's achievements:

> We do not question the great achievements of Chairman Mao, but that does not mean he did not make mistakes. Let's ask:
> 1. Without Mao's support, could Lin Biao have risen?
> 2. Is it possible that Mao did not know Jiang Qing was a conspirator?
> 3. Is it possible that Mao did not know Zhang Chunqiao was a conspirator?

4. Without Mao's support could the Gang of Four have launched the "Antirightist deviationist wind to reverse past verdicts" campaign and dismissed Comrade Deng Xiaoping?

5. Without Mao nodding his head, could the Tian An Men Incident be judged antirevolutionary?

Mao was a human, not a god. We must ascribe to him the status he deserved. Only so can we defend Marxism-Leninism and the Thought of Mao. Without an accurate understanding of Mao, freedom of speech is empty talk. It is the time for all Chinese to shake off the shackles on their thought and behavior.[19]

In applying Deng's precepts to Mao's actions and in invoking Marx and early Mao to refute later Mao, a clever way of demystifying Mao was discovered, one which also undermined the position of those whose political lives depended upon his status.

Deng told foreign visitors that such wall posters were a "normal thing," a "safety valve for the anger of the masses."[20] The anger was apparent, as in one poster which stated that assessments of those responsible for the Cultural Revolution had to be made; to say that Mao was "correct in 70 percent and incorrect in 30 percent" is to shield him, for his mistakes were much greater than people realize.[21]

Deng conceded that some restraint was needed to insure stability; still it was clear that there was a conscious effort to strip Mao down to human size. One by one his deeds were undone. Yao Wenyuan's article, "Comment on The Dismissal of Hai Rui," whose publication was directed by Mao and his wife and considered the first shot of the Cultural Revolution, was condemned in November 1978. The verdict that the Tian An Men Square Incident was counterrevolutionary was reversed to read revolutionary. Peng Dehuai, the defense minister purged in 1959, and Tao Zhu, party propaganda chief purged during the Cultural Revolution, were posthumously rehabilitated. In January 1979 the widow of Liu Shaoqi[22] reappeared in public after ten years of detention foreshadowing the rehabilitation of her husband. At Liu's memorial service on May 17, 1980, Deng called him a "communist saint"—a far cry from his previous designation as a "communist traitor." The rehabilitations of Peng and Liu were clear negations of the Great Leap Forward and the Cultural Revolution.

In September 1979 the third anniversary of Mao's death passed unnoticed. By spring of the following year, most of Mao's portraits in public places had been removed, as had the billboards bearing his quotations at street intersections. In March 1980 the party posthumously attacked Mao's secret service head, Kang Sheng. By mid-year Mao's treasured models of production, the Dazhai agricultural commune and the Daqing oil field, lost their "paragon model" status—Dazhai was declared a failure and Daqing inefficient and unscientific. Even Yenan, Mao's revolutionary cradle (which the author visited in May 1980), was left in a state of benign neglect. It was preserved as a revolutionary shrine of the past while current attention was being focused on the Four Modernizations and their success in the future.

These acts of de-Maoification were outer manifestations of an intense continuous debate within the party over the quality of Mao's leadership and over the assessment of his responsibility. The party had scrutinized Mao's thought in light of "truth according to facts" and, due to his failure to modernize China during his twenty-seven-year rule, gave him an "abstract affirmation but a concrete negation." On the other hand, the "Whateverists"—those who obeyed whatever Mao ordered —still carried Mao's banner and wanted to place revolution in command of modernization. To them, "truth according to facts" was just another of Deng's clever slogans intended to cut down Mao's banner.

Yet the Maoist method was widely viewed as inadequate to meet current challenges. The Deng line, as expressed by the president of the Chinese Academy of Social Sciences, called for the blending of socialist and capitalist ways:

> Only when we merge the superiority of the socialist system with the advanced science and technology of the developed capitalist countries and their advanced managerial experience, only when we combine what is useful in foreign experience

with our own specific conditions and successful experience can we . . . speed up the tempo of the Four Modernizations.[23]

While disagreement over Mao's waning reputation continued, the speech delivered by Marshal Ye on the thirtieth anniversary of the People's Republic on October 1, 1979, was a measured indictment of Mao's leadership and misgovernment:

> Of course, the Mao Zedong Thought is not the product of Mao's personal wisdom alone; it is also the product of the wisdom of his comrades-in-arms, the party, and the revolutionary people. Mao himself had said: "It is the product of the collective struggle of the party and the people."

Surveying the history of the past thirty years, Ye made clear the mistakes committed by the party under Mao's guidance:

> Amidst the immense victories we became imprudent. In 1957, while it was necessary to counterattack a small group of bourgeois rightists, we made the mistake of enlarging the scope [of attack]. In 1958, we violated the principle of carrying out an in-depth investigation, study, and examination of all innovations before giving arbitrary direction, being boastful, and stirring up a "communist storm." In 1959, we improperly carried out the struggle against the so-called right opportunism within the party.

Ye charged that the Cultural Revolution was "the most severe reversal of our socialist cause since the establishment [of the People's Republic] in 1949." Then, pointedly, Ye announced:

> Leaders are not gods. It is impossible for them to be free from mistakes or shortcomings. They should definitely not be deified. We should not play down the role of the collectives and the masses; nor should we indiscriminately exaggerate the role of individual leaders.[24]

In this way the party renounced the personality cult of Mao and moved him from the lofty status of demigod to the humble one of human. Still, an important issue remained unresolved: how far the criticism of Mao should go. In February 1980 Ye made an impassionate plea against a complete repudiation of Mao:

> We can pass resolutions to admit our party's mistakes. We can clear the name of Liu Shaoqi and give him a very high and positive assessment. But we should not reject Mao and dig too deeply into our own cornerstones. . . . The Soviets removed Stalin's tomb, and we whip the corpse of Mao. Wouldn't that prompt people to ask, what is right with socialism and what is good about communism? We can occasionally slap our own faces, but we cannot, nor do we have time to, start from scratch. Those who opposed Mao were not necessarily all wrong, just as those who supported him were not necessarily all right. His opponents and his supporters were all his followers. Was it right or wrong to follow him? Who elevated Mao to such heights and who gave him so much power? Was it the people of the entire country? It was given by the party, the party center, and the army under the leadership of the party. . . . If we want to trace the responsibility to the end, we will find that it lies not with Mao alone. It lies with all of us.[25]

Some took exception to Ye's reasoning, insisting that there was no reason for the party or the people to assume the responsibility of mistakes committed by a single leader. At a time when the country was seeking truth from facts and studying the principle "Practice is the sole criterion of truth," a candid assessment of Mao seemed imperative.[26] Yet Ye's sentiments of moderation were shared by a large segment of party members, especially those in rural areas and those who had joined the party during or after the Cultural Revolution who accounted for half of the 38 million members. They were opposed to harsh criticisms of Mao; he was, after all, human and not a god. Complete repudiation of him would risk negating the party itself.

The central leadership appeared ready to assess Mao's career, but the provinces were more hesitant. To many grass roots party members it was inconceivable to reject the late chairman when a gentle critique would suffice. However, party General Secretary Hu Yaobang made it clear in June 1980 that Mao's thought and economic principles were incompatible with the new historical situation in China.

Certainly, the party would neither deny Mao's contributions nor hide his mistakes, especially his part in the Cultural Revolution, the "decade of great catastrophe." An official assessment of Mao was to be made at the party meetings in mid-1981. Meanwhile, volume five of Mao's *Selected Works* edited by Hua was to be revised, implying dissatisfaction with the editor and with his selections. Thus not only the position of Mao but also that of his anointed successor Hua hung in suspense. The true issues of the post-Mao era appeared to be the three mutually supportive and, indeed, inseparable ones which dominated the period: China's new line, the ascendence of Deng Xiaoping, and the demystification of Mao Zedong.

The de-Maoification of politics is bound to continue as the influence of the thrice-resurrected Deng and his policies for China's modernization begin to be felt in every aspect of Chinese life. Deng's leadership in directing the Four Modernizations will be critical in determining China's future successes.

NOTES

1. Such as General Xu Shiyou and Wei Guoqing, both Politburo members; Xu was also commander of the Guangzhou Military Region, and Wei, party first secretary in Guangtong.
2. *Renmin Ribao* [People's daily], March 19 and 30, 1977. The two letters dated October 10, 1976, and April 10, 1977. For contents, see Richard C. Thornton, "The Political Succession to Mao Tse-tung," *Issues & Studies*, XIV:6:47 (June 1978).
3. Thornton, p. 47.
4. "Communiqué of the Third Plenary Session of the Tenth CCPCC," *Hongqi* [Red flag], No. 8, 1977, p. 6.
5. Hua supporters: Ma Li in Guizhou, Xu Jiadong in Jiangsu, Mao Zhiyong in Hunan, and Song Ping in Gansu.
6. Ye supporters: Su Zhenhua in Shanghai, Tie Ying in Zhejiang, Wang Enmao in Jilin, and Liu Guangtao in Heilongjiang.

7. Deng supporters: Wan Li in Anhui, Huo Shilian in Ninghsia, Jiao Xiaoguang in Guangxi, An Pingsheng in Yunnan, and Tang Qilong in Qinghai.

8. Thornton, pp. 47–49; *Hongqi* [Red flag], No. 8, 1977, pp. 7–8.

9. The breakdown of the three groups was approximately as follows:

The Hua Group	*The Ye Group*	*The Deng Group*
Hua Guofeng	Ye Jianying	Deng Xiaoping
Wang Dongxing	Li Xiannian	Xu Shiyou
Chen Xilian	Xu Xianggian	Wei Guoqing
Wu De	Nie Rongzhen	Peng Chong
Ji Dengkui	Su Zhenhua	Liu Bocheng (old, sick)
Li Desheng		Ulanfu
Chen Yonggui		Geng Biao
Ni Zhifu		Yu Qiuli
Zhang Tingfa		Fang Yi
TOTAL 9	5	9

10. Official Beijing figures quoted in *Central Daily News,* June 30, 1979.

11. Quoted in *The New York Times,* June 19, 1977.

12. *The Christian Science Monitor,* April 27, 1978.

13. Quoted in *The New York Times,* May 17, 1978.

14. *Renmin Ribao* [People's daily], July 1, 1978, p. 3. Tr. mine.

15. "Science and Superstition," *People's Daily,* Oct. 2, 1978. Tr. mine.

16. Quoted in *Central Daily News,* Aug. 5 and 8, 1978.

17. Marx said in his "Theses on Feuerbach": "The question whether objective truth can be attained by human thinking is not a question of theory but is a practical question. It is in practice that man must prove the truth, that is, the reality and power, the temporal nature of his thinking. The dispute over the reality or unreality of thinking which is isolated from practice is a purely scholastic question." See the article, "Practice is the Sole Criterion of Truth," *People's Daily,* May 12, 1978.

18. "Science and Superstition," *Renmin Ribao* [People's daily], Oct. 2, 1978.

19. Reprinted in *Central Daily News,* Jan. 3, 1979. Tr. mine.

20. *Los Angeles Times,* Dec. 2, 1978.

21. *Central Daily News,* Jan. 3, 1979.

22. Wang Guangmei.

23. Hu Qiaomu, "Observe Economic Laws, Speed Up the Four Modernizations," *Peking Review,* No. 45, Nov. 10, 1978, p. 11; see also No. 46, Nov. 17, 1978; No. 47, Nov. 24, 1978.

24. Ye Jianying, "Speech Celebrating the 30th Anniversary of the

Founding of the People's Republic of China," *Renmin Ribao* [People's daily], Sept. 30, 1979. Tr. mine.
25. Reprinted in *Central Daily News*, April 30, 1980. Tr. mine.
26. Statement of Liao Hansheng, political commissar of the Shenyang Military Region.

FURTHER READING

Bush, Richard C., "Deng Xiaoping: China's Old Man in a Hurry," in Robert B. Oxnam and Richard C. Bush (eds.), *China Briefing, 1980* (Boulder, 1980), pp. 9–24.

Chang, Parris H., "The Rise of Wang Tung-hsing: Head of China's Security Apparatus," *The China Quarterly*, 73:122–137 (March 1978).

Chi, Hsin, *Teng Hsiao-ping, A Political Biography* (Hong Kong, 1978).

Ching, Frank, "The Current Political Scene in China," *The China Quarterly*, 80:691–715 (Dec. 1979).

Ch'iu, Hungdah, "China's New Legal System," *Current History*, 79:458:29–32, 44–45 (Sept. 1980).

Cohen, Jerome Alan, "China's Changing Constitution," *The China Quarterly*, 76:794–841 (Dec. 1978).

Dittmer, Lowell, "Death and Transfiguration: Liu Shaoqi's Rehabilitation and Contemporary Chinese Politics," *The Journal of Asian Studies*, XI:3:455–79 (May 1981).

Goldman, Merle, "The Implications of China's Liberalization," *Current History*, 77:449:74–78, 86 (Sept. 1977).

Hua, Guofeng, "Report on the Work of the Government," *Beijing Review*, 27:5–31 (July 6, 1979).

Jain, Jagdish Prasad, *After Mao What? Army Party Group Rivalries in China* (Boulder, 1976).

Kuo, Warren, "The Political Power Structure in Mainland China," *Issues & Studies*, XIV:6:20–31 (June 1978).

Lampton, David M., "China's Succession in Comparative Perspective," *Contemporary China*, III:1:72–79 (Spring 1979).

———, "Politics in the PRC," in Robert B. Oxnam and Richard C. Bush (eds.), *China Briefing, 1980* (Boulder, 1980), pp. 25–37.

Lee, Leo Ou-fan, "Recent Chinese Literature: A Second Hundred Flowers," in Robert B. Oxnam and Richard C. Bush (eds.), *China Briefing, 1980* (Boulder, 1980), pp. 65–73.

Lieberthal, Kenneth, "Modernization and Succession in China," *Contemporary China*, III: 1:53–71 (Spring 1973).

"Man of the Year: Visionary of a New China, Teng Hsiao-p'ing

Opens the Middle Kingdom to the World," *Time* Magazine, Jan. 1, 1979, pp. 13–29.

McDougall, Bonnie S., "Dissent Literature: Official and Nonofficial Literature in and about China in the Seventies," *Contemporary China*, III:4:49–79 (Winter 1979).

McGough, James P., (tr. and ed.), *Fei Hsiao-t'ung: The Dilemma of a Chinese Intellectual* (White Plains, N.Y., 1980).

Montaperto, Ronald N., and Henderson, Jay (eds.), *China's Schools in Flux: Report by the State Education Leaders Delegation, National Committee on United States-China Relations* (White Plains, N.Y., 1980).

Munro, Robin, "Settling Accounts with the Cultural Revolution at Beijing University, 1977–78," *The China Quarterly*, 82:304–333 (June 1980).

National Foreign Assessment Center, *China: A Look at the 11th Central Committee* (Washington, D.C., Oct. 1977).

"On Policy towards Intellectuals," *Beijing Review*, 5:10–15 (Feb. 2, 1979).

Pepper, Suzanne, "An Interview on Changes in Chinese Education after the Gang of Four," *The China Quarterly*, 72:815–824 (Dec. 1977).

———, "Chinese Education After Mao: Two Steps Forward, Two Steps Back and Begin Again," *The China Quarterly*, 81:1–65 (March 1980).

"Premier Hua Reports on the Work of the Government," *Beijing Review*, 25:9–13 (June 22, 1979).

Sullivan, Michael, *The Arts of China*, rev. ed. (Berkeley, 1978).

———, "Painting with a New Brush: Art in Post-Mao China," in Robert B. Oxnam and Richard C. Bush (eds.), *China Briefing, 1980* (Boulder, 1980), pp. 53–63.

Teng Hsiao-ping and the "General Program" (San Francisco, 1977).

"The Communiqué of the Third Plenum of the Tenth Central Committee of the Chinese Communist Party," full text in Chinese in *Hongqi* [Red flag], 8:5–9, (1977).

Thornton, Richard C., "The Political Succession to Mao Tse-tung," *Issues & Studies*, XIV:6:32–52 (June 1978).

Wakeman, Frederic, Jr., "Historiography in China after Smashing the Gang of Four," *The China Quarterly*, 76:891–911 (Dec. 1978).

3

The Normalization of Relations
between China
and the United States

Following the Nixon visit to Beijing in 1972, there was a conspicuous lack of progress in Sino-American relations due to unfavorable conditions in both countries. In China the radical Gang of Four, experiencing the heights of their influence, were scheming to seize power in hopes of succeeding Mao; their line was firmly antiforeign and suspicious of any rapprochement with the capitalist Americans. In the United States, recognition of China faltered on the Taiwan issue as Beijing insisted on the fulfillment of three conditions: (1) terminate diplomatic relations with the Republic of China on Taiwan, (2) abrogate the United States–Taiwan defense treaty of 1954, and (3) withdraw all American forces from Taiwan. In a global perspective, to accede to these conditions might be perceived as abandoning Taiwan and cast doubt on the credibility of American commitments to other allies. The Taiwan issue had become a mirror of America's international self-image, and thus its resolution took on added significance beyond the problems of normalization.

President Nixon was reportedly prepared to recognize Beijing, but was kept from doing so by the Watergate scandal.

His political survival came to depend increasingly on the support of conservatives in Congress who opposed normalization, and the preservation of his presidency seemed far more urgent than the diplomatic recognition of China. He was too deeply mired in the fight for his political life to take action on China.[1]

After Nixon's resignation, interim President Gerald Ford was first immobilized by the debacle of Vietnam's collapse and then by his growing aspirations to seek election in 1976. Though in favor of normalization in principle, Ford, too, realized his need for conservative support and made no moves toward recognizing China. Jimmy Carter, Ford's successor, also favored normalization in principle, but his first year in office was occupied with the Panama Canal Treaties, Strategic Arms Limitation Talks with the Soviets (SALT II), Russian-Cuban activities in Africa, and the Middle East problems. These pressing issues required the support of the conservatives in Congress who often considered themselves "friends of Taiwan."

Indeed, Taiwan became a sensitive issue in American domestic politics standing tenaciously in the way of normalization. American public opinion opposed breaking relations with Taiwan, although it favored the recognition of China.[2] The problem before the United States became one of safeguarding Taiwan if normalization were to occur. Politicians agreed that if arms sales to Taiwan could continue, the United States would not appear to be abandoning a faithful ally, and this would minimize the questions of America's credibility and its commitments to other countries.

An easing of the domestic conditions in both countries was necessary before either would feel ready to move toward normalization. Ultimately, the breakthrough came largely as a result of changes in Chinese policy. These changes came in the form of subtle concessions for which three American presidents had waited for nearly seven years.

THE NORMALIZATION OF DIPLOMATIC RELATIONS

During the three years following Watergate and the resignation of President Nixon, the Chinese had frequently expressed impatience with the lack of progress toward normalization. President Carter saw no urgent reason to accommodate Beijing, especially when he could not seem to find an expedient solution to the Taiwan issue. However, he experienced increasing pressure from his national security advisor, foreign policy staff, and liberal Democrats to jettison formal ties with Taiwan in favor of recognizing China. Biding his time, Carter dispatched Secretary of State Cyrus Vance on an "exploratory mission" to Beijing, in reality a mission of "contact" without substance.

Vance's Visit

Vance was in China from August 21 to 25, 1977. Although he was the first high official of the Carter administration to visit China, the Chinese gave him a lukewarm reception—even the food at the welcoming banquet was unexceptional by Chinese standards, and the occasion was marked by the absence of any Politburo member.[3] Vance did, however, discuss a wide range of subjects with Foreign Minister Huang Hua, Vice-Premier Deng Xiaoping, and Chairman Hua Guofeng. On the issue of Taiwan, Vance suggested the establishment of an American embassy in Beijing and a liaison office in Taipei; but the Chinese rejected the idea, insisting on the fulfillment of the three conditions previously mentioned. The issue of continued American arms sales to Taiwan after normalization was not even discussed.[4] The Chinese would not commit themselves to a nonviolent method of liberating Taiwan, with Hua reaffirming: "Taiwan province is China's sacred province. We are determined to liberate Taiwan. When and how is entirely an internal affair of China, which brooks no foreign interference whatsoever."

To no one's surprise, Vance returned empty-handed. From

the American perspective, the mission ventured little and gained little. With the Panama Canal Treaties before Congress for ratification, Washington saw no need for "hasty" action on China. The Chinese, however, considered the meeting a step backward in Chinese-American relations.

Brzezinski's Visit

If Vance's reception in China was less than effusive, the visit made by National Security Advisor Zbigniew Brzezinski (May 20–22, 1978) was a study in contrast. As Washington perceived in the Soviet paranoia of a Sino-American axis a powerful weapon for SALT negotiations, concessions to China were suddenly rendered "practical." Brzezinski's mission was to seek upgrading in Chinese-American relations. Before his departure from Washington, D.C., he declared openly that the United States wanted to expand relations with China and make progress toward full normalization. Washington also let it be known that it was ready to accede to the three Chinese demands, while expecting China not to take Taiwan by force and not to object to continued American arms sales to Taiwan after normalization. Thus the Chinese knew in advance of Brzezinski's mission and welcomed him warmly.

In Beijing, Brzezinski announced: "The president of the United States desires friendly relations with a strong China. He is determined to join you in overcoming the remaining obstacles in the way of full normalization of our relations." He remarked that the United States shared China's resolve to "resist the efforts of any nation which seeks to establish global or regional hegemony," adding that "neither of us dispatches international marauders who masquerade as non-aligned to advance big-power ambitions in Africa. Neither of us seeks to enforce the political obedience of our neighbors through military force."[5] The Chinese were delighted with Brzezinski's statements, which clearly maligned both the Russians and the Cubans while intentionally echoing China's own world view. They were all the more pleased because the timing of the visit, May

20, coincided with the inauguration of Chiang Ching-kuo as president of the Nationalist government and was therefore considered a deliberate snub to Taiwan.

Brzezinski returned again and again to the themes of the Soviet threat to world peace and the shared interests of China and the United States in world affairs. Climbing the Great Wall he jested with the accompanying Chinese: "If we get to the top first, you go in and oppose the Russians in Ethiopia. If you get there first, we go in and oppose the Russians in Ethiopia." Having reached the top he joked again: "I was looking but I did not see the polar bear."[6] Such spontaneous but pointed antics were calculated to win the Chinese favor.

Brzezinski briefed the Chinese leaders on the status of SALT II and on the American views of the world situation in order to emphasize that the "long term strategic nature of the United States relationship to China . . . based on certain congruence of fundamental interests" was of an enduring nature. To demonstrate American sincerity, Brzezinski divulged to the Chinese the contents of two secret documents: Presidential Review Memorandum 10 (the U.S. assessment of the world situation), and Presidential Directive 18 (the president's security policy implementation plan). Other American experts consulted with their Chinese counterparts on defense, technology, and bilateral relations.

Although no public announcement was made on normalization, Brzezinski privately informed Hua and Deng that Ambassador Leonard Woodcock would be ready to begin serious negotiations to that end.[7] Satisfied with Brzezinski's visit, the Chinese called it "two steps forward." Later, a member of the Standing Committee of the National People's Congress[8] hinted that if the United States accepted China's three conditions, Beijing would not be likely to attack Taiwan and the normalization could materialize during the Carter administration.[9] Such a statement, though not an official one, seemed an indication of China's willingness to compromise on Taiwan in order to ensure American recognition. In Washington, the ratification of the Panama Canal Treaties cleared the way for President Carter to act more decisively on China.

Toward Normalization

In July 1978 the Carter administration sent an influential scientific and technological mission to China under the leadership of Dr. Frank Press, the president's advisor on science and technology. Dr. Press returned home in mid-July with the report that the Chinese had requested to send students to the United States immediately, rather than waiting for Washington to break relations with Taiwan as they had previously insisted. The Carter administration took this subtle concession as a sign of new flexibility on the part of Beijing.

On September 19 Carter received the new head of the Chinese Liaison Office, Ambassador Chai Zemin, and offered him a proposal for normalization on the basis of three conditions: (1) continued American commercial and cultural ties with Taiwan; (2) the American resolve that the Taiwan-China problem should be peacefully solved; and (3) continued American arms sales to Taiwan after normalization.[10]

In October Carter made his most important decision concerning normalization. Feeling politically secure after his success as a mediator in the Camp David peace talks between Egyptian President Anwar el-Sadat and Israeli Prime Minister Begin, the president decided he could finally afford to break America's commitments to Taiwan and set January 1, 1979, as the deadline for diplomatic recognition of China. It was calculated that by that time the Egyptian-Israeli treaty would have been signed, and in its euphoric wake any criticism of the handling of Taiwan would be defused.[11] On the other hand, if the Middle East agreement failed, a successful normalization with China would serve to assure the American electorate of Carter's statesmanship as a world leader. The president wanted to appear decisive, to use China to speed up the SALT negotiations with the Russians, and to outplay liberal advocates of China's recognition such as Senator Edward Kennedy.[12]

Woodcock, the former president of the United States Automobile Workers, was an experienced and skillful negotiator. In November he presented to the Beijing government the draft of a joint communiqué to which the Chinese responded by asking for certain clarifications. Then, unexpectedly, Vice-Premier Deng announced that he would like to visit the United States— a signal of his willingness to deal. On December 4, the Chinese presented their version of a joint communiqué, and on December 11 Deng was officially invited to the United States.

On December 13 Deng received Woodcock, who said, "Mr. Deputy Premier, I have in my pocket a short communiqué which I'm authorized to show you if you want to see it." Deng had the text translated instantly and responded, "We'll accept that. . . . We cannot accept that. . . . This is nicely put. . . . How about changing this part?"[13] The two met four times in the next two days, and on December 15 Deng said: "We will never agree to your selling arms to Taiwan, but we will set that aside in order to achieve normalization."[14] With this "agreement to disagree," the stage was set for a formal announcement of normalization.[15]

On December 15, 1978, a somber President Carter made a hastily arranged television appearance to announce that the United States and the People's Republic of China had agreed to establish full diplomatic relations on January 1, 1979, including the exchange of ambassadors and the establishment of embassies on the following March 1. The United States would break official relations with Taiwan and abrogate the 1954 Mutual Defense Treaty on January 1, 1980, in accordance with the treaty's termination provision that one year's advance notice was required. The president pledged that Taiwan "won't be sacrificed": the United States would continue to maintain commercial, cultural, and other relations with Taiwan through informal representatives, and the relationship would include arms sales. Then, with obvious exhilaration, he announced that Vice-Premier Deng would visit the United States in January 1979.

In announcing normalization, Carter cited the achievement of Presidents Nixon and Ford showing that normalization had been a bipartisan objective in hopes that conservative criticism would be minimized. Fortunately for him, the "China lobby" had waned so much that it could mount only a feeble protest to normalization. The majority of Americans, while regretting "dumping" the Nationalist government on Taiwan, found it hard to oppose the simple mathematics of the possibility of relations with 900 million people on mainland China compared with the 17 million on Taiwan.[16] In bringing normalization to fruition, Carter projected the image of a determined president and politically he gained more than he lost in popular support.[17]

Simultaneously in Beijing Chairman Hua called an unprecedented news conference for foreign and Chinese journalists to announce the normalization. He specifically pointed out that China did not like the continued American sales of arms to, and maintenance of cultural and commercial links with, Taiwan, but it would not let these issues stand in the way of normalization. "We can absolutely not agree to this. . . . The continued sale of arms to Taiwan by the United States does not conform to the principles of normalization and would be detrimental to the peaceful solution of the issue of Taiwan. . . . Nonetheless, we reached agreement on the joint communiqué."

The salient features of the joint communiqué are as follows:[18]

1. The United States of America and the People's Republic of China have agreed to recognize each other and to establish diplomatic relations as of January 1, 1979.
2. The United States recognizes the government of the People's Republic of China as the sole legal government of China. Within this context, the people of the United States will maintain cultural, commercial, and other unofficial relations with the people of Taiwan.
3. The United States and China reaffirm the principles agreed to by the two sides in the Shanghai Communiqué and emphasize again that:
   a. Both wish to reduce the danger of international military conflict.
   b. Neither should seek hegemony in the Asia-Pacific region

or in any other region of the world and each is opposed to efforts by any other country or group of countries to establish such hegemony.

c. Neither is prepared to negotiate on behalf of any third party or to enter into agreements or understandings with the other directed at other states.

d. The United States acknowledges the Chinese position that there is but one China and Taiwan is part of China.

e. Both believe that normalization of Sino-American relations is not only in the interest of the Chinese and American peoples but also contributes to the cause of peace in Asia and the world.

4. The United States and China will exchange Ambassadors and establish Embassies on March 1, 1979.

Separately, the United States issued a statement on Taiwan:[19]

1. On that same date, January 1, 1979, the United States will notify Taiwan that it is terminating diplomatic relations and that the Mutual Defense Treaty between the United States and the Republic of China is being terminated in accordance with the provisions of the Treaty. The United States also states that it will be withdrawing its remaining military personnel from Taiwan within four months.

2. In the future, the American people and the people of Taiwan will maintain commercial, cultural, and other relations without official government representation and without diplomatic relations.

3. The United States is confident that the people of Taiwan face a peaceful and prosperous future. The United States continues to have an interest in the peaceful resolution of the Taiwan issue and expects that the Taiwan issue will be settled peacefully by the Chinese themselves.

Obviously, the initiative for breaking the Taiwan issue came from China with Deng as the chief mover. Normalization would give him the success that had eluded Mao and Zhou, facilitate his visit to the United States, increase trade, and make available to the Chinese American science, technology, capital, and credit. In this light, Taiwan paled into relative insignificance. In any case, China was well aware it lacked the naval capacity to launch an attack on the island and was clearly too absorbed in the Four Modernizations to want a costly, nasty, and prolonged war over Taiwan. Accepting the status quo was expedient because it gave China an American recognition of its title to Taiwan, though not immediate possession of it.[20]

Beijing accepted the new view that China's relations with the United States were more important than Taiwan in the present world setting. The Soviet-Vietnamese treaty of November 1978 with its overtones of military alliance might have prodded the Chinese to seek a closer tie with the United States. Ironically, China's growing preoccupation with its two erstwhile allies may have prompted its rapprochement with its former enemies in the West. It is even possible that China was already contemplating a military confrontation with Vietnam over the worsening situation in Cambodia, and that it was counting on a friendly United States to deter Soviet involvement. At any rate, the Soviet press blasted away at China's motives in seeking American and Western connections.

Meanwhile, in Taiwan, the government had been given barely a few hours' notice of the normalization announcements. President Chiang bitterly vowed that his government would neither negotiate with the communist Chinese government nor compromise with communism. Some 2,000 angry people vented their wrath by besieging the American Embassy and burning the American flag.

In the United States, by contrast, responses were generally favorable. *The Los Angeles Times* editorialized, "No Sinful Sellout"; *The Christian Science Monitor*, "China: It Had To Come"; and *The New York Times*, "The Cost of Stalling on China."[21] The politicians, as usual, were divided: liberal Republicans and Democrats generally supported recognition, while conservatives such as former California Governor Ronald Reagan condemned it as a betrayal; Senator Barry Goldwater called it "one of the most cowardly acts by any president in history." Threatening to sue the president for violating the constitution in abrogating the Taiwan defense treaty, Goldwater insisted that legally the president must consult the Senate to terminate a treaty. Conservative opposition to recognition soon centered on Goldwater's legal action against the president.

Relations with Taiwan

To soften the blow to Taiwan, Carter sent a high-level delegation to Taipei on December 27, 1978, led by Deputy Secretary of State Warren Christopher.[22] He carried the message that despite the termination of formal relations, the United States hoped that trade and cultural ties would continue to expand. The Americans were greeted by 10,000 demonstrators who beat on the sides of the limousines, splashed red paint and hurled eggs, mud, and tomatoes. Other mobs trampled heaps of peanuts under their feet, to show their feelings about Carter by attacking the source of his family business.

President Chiang told the delegation that his government and people were enraged by Washington's failure to consult Taipei in advance of the agreement with Beijing. He insisted that future relations between Taiwan and the United States be conducted on a government-to-government basis, that his government be recognized as the one in actual control of Taiwan, and that it would continue to present itself as the legal government of China. The Americans, however, were only prepared to negotiate a framework for unofficial, non-governmental contacts. Two days of attempts at talks ended inconclusively, and the delegation returned home with nothing resolved.

American ties with Taiwan were extremely complex. Apart from the defense treaty, the United States maintained fifty-nine lesser treaties and agreements with the government of the Republic of China. These protected the special relationship of the two countries in agricultural commodities, atomic energy, aviation, claims, controlled drugs, economic and technical cooperation, education, investment guarantees, maritime matters, postal matters, taxation, and trade and commerce.[23]

American investment in Taiwan was considerable. Leading

American corporations doing business in Taiwan included such giants as Bank of America, Chase Manhattan Bank, Citicorp, American Express, Ford, RCA, Union Carbide, Zenith, and Corning Glass. In 1978, 220 American corporations had over 500 million dollars invested in Taiwan.[24] Taiwan enjoyed a brisk foreign trade of $23.7 billion in 1978, and a third of it ($7.3 billion) was American. Obviously, American economic ties with Taiwan could not be easily reduced; if anything, they were expected to continue to expand, regardless of withdrawal of diplomatic recognition. Japan's trade with Taiwan had grown 233 percent after it normalized relations with Beijing; Australia's, 370 percent; and Canada's, 539 percent.[25] Similar growth in America's trade with Taiwan seemed a reasonable expectation.

Regarding arms sales to Taiwan, the Pentagon prepared a sixty-page confidential document (Consolidated Guidance 9) which assessed Taiwan's military needs. It recommended that the United States continue military links with Taiwan to protect its armed forces from falling into disarray. Contracts already signed for spare parts and military equipment were to be honored, including a vast array of highly specialized bombs and missiles as well as more conventional equipment. The document called for accelerated arms sales to show Congress that the United States was not totally abandoning Taiwan. The Pentagon considered Taiwan able to repel an enemy attack as long as the United States provided air support, and continued arms and parts sales. With 500,000 men in its regular armed forces and a militia of 2 million, Taiwan's self-defense capabilities were ample though ultimately still dependent on the United States for its key weapon systems.[26]

After an initial spasm of angry outrage, Taiwan's leaders calmed down and weathered the political storm with dignity, dedication, and self-reliance. The sixty-eight-year-old President Chiang told his people on December 24, 1978: "We must undertake careful review, think things out soberly, and design our counter-measures with special calm and prudence to advance and carry out our policy and reach our goal."[27] Taiwan's leaders realized they could not afford to irritate the United States too much, for the American tie, albeit unofficial, was a vital one.

Since the American embassy in Taipei, and the Republic of China embassy in Washington were scheduled to close on March 1, 1979, it was imperative that substitute offices be designated to handle continuing relations. The Nationalist government struggled for some sort of official status, while the American negotiators insisted on unofficial relations. On February 15, 1979, it was finally agreed that there should be an American Institute in Taipei to replace the embassy and a Coordinating Council for North American Affairs in Washington, D.C., to take care of Taiwan's interests, with consulate-like branches in nine major cities. The American Institute would be staffed by "retired" State Department and other government personnel who would work without official titles.

Meanwhile, Congress produced a number of resolutions expressing concerns for the future of Taiwan. One offered by Senators Kennedy and Cranston directed the president to inform Congress of "any danger to the interests, concerns, and expectations of the United States in the peace, prosperity, and welfare of Taiwan," and to meet such danger "in accordance with constitutional processes and procedures established by law." On March 10, 1979, the Senate and the House overwhelmingly supported two slightly different versions of the legislation (the American-Chinese Relations Act, or the Taiwan Relations Act) ratifying the normalization of relations with China and approving the machinery for unofficial relations with Taiwan. The legislation spelled out American determination to maintain extensive relations with the people of Taiwan and "to consider any effort to resolve the Taiwan issue by other than peaceful means a threat to the peace and security of the Western Pacific area and of grave concern to the United States." Passing two versions of the bill necessitated a compromise by a joint conference committee, and the final bill was passed in the Senate (85 to 4) and the House (339 to 50) on March 28.

Beijing protested the language of the bill and charged that

it treated Taiwan as if it were a sovereign state, even though all documents would be revised to refer to "the people of Taiwan" rather than the government. By Beijing's definition, "the people" included the "governing authorities on Taiwan." It also asked that the former Nationalist embassy in Washington, which had been turned over to a private organization called The Friends of Free China, and other holdings be designated the legal properties of the People's Republic of China.

In spite of China's dissatisfaction with the tone of the normalizaiton proceedings, they had moved with surprising smoothness. There still remained the lawsuit of Goldwater and twenty-five associates challenging the constitutionality of Carter's termination of the Taiwan defense treaty. They won a favorable ruling from the United States District Court on October 17, 1979, but lost in both the Appeals and Supreme Courts, which ruled that the treaty termination in question was "non-judicial and political in nature" and dictated by "a traumatic change in international circumstances."[28]

The Vietnamese Invasion of Cambodia

An unacknowledged but possible repercussion of normalization was the Vietnamese invasion of Cambodia under Soviet patronage. Relations between Vietnam and Cambodia had been deteriorating, and in November 1978 Vietnam and Russia had signed what was, in effect, a military alliance. The American announcement of recognition of China was followed ten days later by the Vietnamese invasion of Cambodia. On January 7, 1979, after a chillingly effective blitzkrieg of fifteen days, the Vietnamese forces took the Cambodian capital of Phnom Penh, destroying the Chinese-supported Pol Pot regime. Cambodia appealed to the United Nations Security Council for intervention while Beijing took the invasion as proof of Soviet hegemony in Asia and moved troops toward its border with Vietnam.

While a cause-and-effect relationship between American recognition of China and the Vietnamese invasion of Cambodia was impossible to prove, many secretly opined that normalization had goaded the Soviets and the Vietnamese into action against Cambodia.[29] China faced the difficult decision of how to deal with the aggressors. Deng's visit to the United States would surely help the Chinese assess the American position.

Deng's Visit

China's dynamic, diminutive senior Vice-Premier Deng Xiaoping flew into Washington, D.C., on January 28, 1979, for a nine-day visit. This being the first visit by a senior official from the People's Republic of China in thirty years, it warranted a more lavish and regal reception than Washington usually provided. Though ranked third on China's official protocol list, Deng was beyond doubt China's most powerful leader. Washington was anxious for him to see the country, to get a sense of its creativity and diversity, and to understand the important role Congress plays in the formulation of national policy. The administration secretly hoped that Deng would speak softly on Taiwan and not make statements irritating to the Soviets.

The first day after his arrival, Deng was officially welcomed on the White House lawn with a nineteen-gun salute and review of the honor guard. Hailing the visit as a "time of reunion and new beginnings" for the two countries, President Carter said; "It is a day of reconciliation when windows too long closed have been reopened." Deng was gracious in his response but would not let the occasion pass without a veiled attack on the Soviet Union: "The world today is far from tranquil. There are not only threats to peace, but the factors causing war are visibly growing." Following the formal welcome, the two leaders and their aides conferred privately for four hours.

At the White House dinner reception attended by hundreds of corporate executives, members of Congress, and other prominent Americans, Carter said: "We have a long-term commitment to a world of diverse and independent nations. We believe that a strong and secure China will play a cooperative part in that community." Deng's reply contained another oblique but unmistakable swipe at the Soviet threat to world peace: "In the joint communiqué on the establishment of diplomatic relations, our two sides solemnly committed ourselves that neither should seek hegemony and each was opposed to efforts by any other country or group of countries to establish such hegemony." Carter, somewhat ill at ease, smiled weakly over his guest's veiled references to Moscow.

After the glittering dinner party, the group moved to the Kennedy Center Opera House for an evening of American music and dance and the basketball wizardry of the Harlem Globetrotters. It was Deng, however, who was the evening's biggest hit. Charming performers and audience alike, he went on stage to shake hands and kiss the foreheads of the children in a choir very much in the style of an American politician running for office. Vice-President Mondale quipped, "It's a good thing you're not an American citizen, because you'd be elected to any office you sought."[30]

In meetings with senators and representatives, Deng took Capitol Hill by storm. On Taiwan he indicated that China no longer used the expression "liberation" but only "unification" with the motherland:

> Until Taiwan is returned and there is only one China, we will fully respect the realities on Taiwan. We will permit the present system on Taiwan and its way of life to remain unchanged. We will allow the local government of Taiwan to maintain people-to-people relations with other people like Japan and the United States. With this policy we believe we can achieve peaceful means of unification. We Chinese have patience. However, China cannot commit herself not to resort to other means.

This was reassuring to legislators like Senator Henry Jackson who would have preferred stronger assurances of nonviolence, but respected Deng's caution in exercising China's options.

As for the Soviet Union, Deng's criticism was stinging. Though not opposed to any strategic arms agreement the United States might reach with the Soviet Union, he stressed, "You can't trust the Russians," bringing nods of agreement from the lawmakers. When alone with newsmen Deng was more forceful in denouncing the Soviets, urging the formation of a common front between the United States, Japan, Western Europe, and China to block Russian expansion the world over. He condemned Soviet support of Vietnam's invasion of Cambodia and suggested that the United States denounce both of them, or at least the Vietnamese, those "Cubans of the Orient," who, Deng insisted, "must be taught some necessary lessons."

With respect to the most-favored-nation status for Chinese trade, Deng noted the Jackson-Vanik amendment, which denied such status to countries that did not permit free emigration, and said with a chuckle: "This is no problem to us. But do you really want 10 million Chinese (to move to the United States)?" This was met with a burst of laughter and perhaps some relief. No one could resist Deng's sense of humor.

Deng played the role of a goodwill ambassador superbly. He struck up a warm friendship with Carter and managed to charm Congress with his quick wit, humor, and controlled self-confidence. His adroit showmanship—shaking hands, hugging, kissing, beaming, laughing, and teasing—endeared him to the American public, persuading them that in a cowboy hat even a Communist was hard to hate. The Chinese people, via television satellite, followed Deng's every movement with pride and delight. The blunt, feisty, irascible man many reporters had portrayed was nowhere to be seen. Deng projected himself as a warm human being rather than as a fiery revolutionary. He made it clear that while China might be poor and backward, it was no international beggar. It needed foreign technology and capital but could also offer a rewarding market for American products. Partly because of Deng's captivating personality and mastery of mass psychology, and partly because of America's taste for the novel and tendency to glamorize new celebrities, Deng's striking success opened the mind and heart of America to the People's Republic of China.

Perhaps an equally constructive, if less tangible, part of the visit was Deng's personal observation of the workings of American democracy and of the operations of a modern economy. The executive branch, though powerful, had its limitations, and Deng witnessed Congress's distinct role in forming national policy. In visits to a Ford assembly plant, the Hughes Tool Company, and the Johnson Space Center, Deng saw the efficiency of American business operations which with space-age technology and hardworking employees could provide the clearly comfortable American standard of living. It is possible that much of what Deng learned could prove useful in shaping China's future.

Deng's key message to the United States—the Soviet threat and the need for a common front against it—received only a polite response. Clearly, the security concerns of the United States did not coincide exactly with those of China. In reality Deng's warnings alerted many Americans to the danger of being drawn inadvertently into undesirable situations. There were renewed calls for balanced relations with both China and the Soviet Union, not allowing either to maneuver the United States into a confrontation with the other.[31]

Deng himself was satisfied with the results of his trip. He and Foreign Minister Huang Hua signed three agreements with Carter and Vance on science and technology, cultural exchanges, and consular relations. The last permitted China to establish consulates in San Francisco and Houston, and the United States to do the same in Guangzhou and Shanghai. In a farewell message to Carter, Deng said that the visit was a "complete success" and expressed the belief that Chinese-American relations "will witness major progress under the new historical conditions." Deng's optimism was surpassed only by the excitement and hopes of the American and Chinese peoples, who can now view one another more freely and with open interest for the first time in thirty years.

The Chinese Invasion of Vietnam

On February 17, 1979, barely a week after Deng's return, a large Chinese invasion force struck into Vietnam. In name the invasion was in retaliation for numerous Vietnamese incursions into China, but in fact it was China's punishment for Vietnam's invasion of Cambodia and for its blatant ingratitude after it had accepted more than twenty-five years of Chinese assistance.

As early as 1950 Mao had offered Ho Chi Minh military, political, and economic aid—the famous battle of Dienbienfu (1954) was fought largely with Chinese weapons and under Chinese direction. During the height of American involvement in Vietnam (1964–71), China dispatched 300,000 technical personnel and troops to Vietnam to help in air defense, engineering work, railway construction, road repairs, and logistics supplies; some 10,000 of them lost their lives. Chinese economic aid to Vietnam between 1950 and 1978 totaled somewhere between $15–20 billion, which represented considerable Chinese sacrifice.[32]

For all these acts of friendship, China had expected Vietnam's gratitude and goodwill but received precious little once Hanoi gained control over all Vietnam. Perhaps fearful of China's vast influence, Vietnam rejected its dependence on China and turned instead to the Russians for help. Gradually, increasing mistreatment of Chinese residents in Vietnam and of Vietnamese of Chinese descent was followed by a wave of persecution, and 160,000 of them were forced to flee. The crowning insult was Vietnam's conclusion of a Twenty-five-year Friendship and Mutual Defense Treaty with Russia, which served the Soviet purpose of encircling China and represented a stinging Vietnamese rejection of Beijing. China's patience was strained beyond tolerance by Vietnam's invasion of Laos and Cambodia, and the consequent collapse of the Chinese-supported Pol Pot regime.

During his stay in Washington, Deng openly spoke of "teaching the Vietnamese some necessary lessons," but he never specified the type of action China might take. Carter tried to dissuade him from military action but evoked no positive response; Chinese build-up on the Vietnamese border continued. On February 8, 1979, Moscow warned Beijing against "overstepping the forbidden line," and a few days later Vietnam called on "all friendly nations" to stop China from waging war against it.

The Chinese wanted a quick war—a repeat of their invasion

into India in 1962—lightening success and rapid retreat before the Russians could decide on a proper response. It was a calculated risk which Deng thought worth taking. With China's new international connections he anticipated no Soviet military intervention. To calm world public opinion, China declared at the outset of the invasion that it would be a limited operation of short duration, with no design on Vietnamese territory.

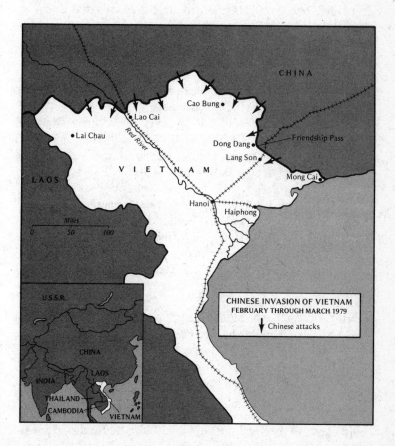

CHINESE INVASION OF VIETNAM
FEBRUARY THROUGH MARCH 1979
↓ Chinese attacks

The magnitude of the Chinese invasion, involving 250,000 troops and hundreds of tanks, fighter planes, and artillery striking in ten directions along a 450-mile front, suggested a well-prepared military operation. The Chinese forces advanced swiftly and successfully at first, taking four Vietnamese provincial capitals near the border by the end of a week.[33] However, their movement was soon slowed considerably, due largely to the lack of modern weapons. The Chinese had hoped to draw the enemy forces into a major battle and destroy them decisively, but the Vietnamese deliberately avoided a direct confrontation. Of Vietnam's 600,000 troops, about two-thirds were stationed in Cambodia and South Vietnam performing "occupation duties." Rather than risk the security of these areas by removing troops, Vietnam's plan was to employ only regional forces and militia to fight the Chinese, thereby preserving its best troops from annihilation.

As the war dragged on, the prospect for a quick Chinese success faded and the danger of Soviet retaliation increased correspondingly. In an apparent attempt to appease international worries about escalation and possible Soviet intervention, Beijing declared that it had no intention of attacking Hanoi. The world community remained concerned, and the United Nations Security Council called for Chinese withdrawal from Vietnam and Vietnamese withdrawal from Cambodia, though the potential of a Soviet or Chinese veto prevented the resolution's passage. The United States "regretted" the outbreak of war but considered its national interests unjeopardized. It ruled out any use of force "except under the most extreme, compelling circumstances," meaning Soviet intervention. The Soviets mobilized troops on the Chinese border and Outer Mongolia called up reserve forces to put pressure on China, but there were no signs of imminent intervention.

On March 1 the Chinese proposed peace talks while stepping up their costly assault on Lang Son. There was a general belief, or even hope, that once the Chinese overran Lang Son, they could claim victory and return home. By March 2 the city was in utter ruins, and the Vietnamese abandoned it to take positions in the surrounding hills. The Chinese finally took Lang

Son, but the victory was far from resounding. Rather, it was labored, protracted, and unspectacular—a far cry from the lightening blitz that the Chinese had dreamed of. By this time Cuba had offered to send troops to Vietnam, and Russia had warned China to halt its "brazen bandit attack" and evacuate Vietnam immediately. Having taken nearly all the important towns and provincial capitals in northern Vietnam, China declared its objectives fulfilled and called for a ceasefire.

The Vietnamese refused to acknowledge defeat, boasting that their best troops were still intact and capable of defeating any Chinese invasion. Moreover, they claimed that the Chinese had placed themselves in a no-win situation when they announced that the war was to be a short, limited operation. In an amusing but crude way, Hanoi said: "If the Chinese win, they lose. If they lose, they lose. If they withdraw, it is a Vietnamese victory." On March 5 Beijing announced the withdrawal of its troops after seventeen days of fighting, and on the following day Hanoi agreed to hold peace talks. By March 16 the Chinese had completed their withdrawal.

Western military experts wondered why China risked so much, including military confrontation with the Soviets, for so little. They failed to see that China felt both humiliated and betrayed in its rejection by a former supplicant of favors, and that the feeling of betrayal was exacerbated by Vietnam's growing arrogance toward China and other smaller neighbors, as well as by its alignment with Russia. Such open hostility, the Chinese felt, had to be dealt with, or China's credibility would be at stake. As Deng stated, China wanted to teach the Vietnamese that "they could not run about as much as they desired. . . . They controlled Laos, invaded Cambodia, signed a peace treaty with the Soviet Union that was essentially a military alliance, and encroached on Chinese soil as well." Deng also wanted to show the world that China did not fear war or the threat of Soviet intervention. Fortunately, his assessment of the situation turned out to be correct, and China gained some satisfaction in exposing the Soviet Union as a "paper tiger."

If China taught Vietnam a lesson, it also learned one: that

China could not fight a modern war effectively without streamlining the military and that the economic consequences of war
could be disastrous. In the seventeen-day operation, China
sustained 46,000 casualties, lost 400 tanks and armored vehicles,
and spent $1.36 billion. Draining the country's scarce resources
had an immediate and adverse effect on the Four Modernizations, necessitating a cutback in the 1980 military budget by
1.9 billion. At the same time, the goal of scientific and technological modernization of the military became increasingly
imperative.

THE NORMALIZATION OF TRADE
AND OTHER RELATIONS

The diplomatic recognition of China was followed by a series
of negotiations for the normalization of commercial, cultural,
scientific, and to some extent even military relations. China
lacked the most-favored-nation status, making it extremely
difficult for Chinese exports to the United States to be competitive. For Washington to grant China this status, it was
necessary to settle the question of blocked American assets in
China and of frozen Chinese assets in the United States.

Claims Settlement and the Trade Pact

The day after the American liaison office in Beijing became an
official embassy on March 1, 1979, Treasury Secretary Michael
Blumenthal, who had lived in Shanghai as a youth, initialed
an agreement with Chinese Minister of Finance Zhang Jingfu
settling the disputes of "frozen assets and blocked claims."
The disputes dated back to the early years of the Korean War
when in 1950, responding to China's entry into the war, President Truman froze $80.5 million in Chinese assets in the United
States. China retaliated by seizing property in China owned
by American churches, corporations, schools, and individuals
valued at $196.9 million. In reality, the American property in
question had been in Chinese hands since the establishment

of the People's Republic in October 1949. There were 384 American claims, the largest coming from the Boise Cascade Corporation.

The agreement initialed in Beijing allowed China to retain the American property but pay $80.5 million to settle the total American claims—roughly 41 cents on the dollar. China was to pay $30 million on October 1, 1979, and the rest in installments of $10.1 million each October until 1984. For its part, the United States would "unfreeze" the $80.5 million in Chinese assets, but it was not known how much of it belonged to the Chinese government and how much to banks, corporations, schools, and individuals, both inside and outside of China. A noteworthy point, rarely seen in international settlements, was that the Chinese payment, though equal to the amount of the frozen assets, was not tied to them—American claimants would receive their reimbursements quickly. It appears to be a favorable agreement when compared with other such international settlements, and its compensations were more favorable than the Americans might have hoped for.[34]

The initialed accord had only to be officially signed by representatives of the two governments and was not subject to Congressional ratification. To sign the accord and to negotiate a new trade agreement, Washington sent Secretary of Commerce Juanita Kreps to China. On May 11, 1979, she signed the agreement on "frozen assets-blocked claims" with Chinese Finance Minister Zhang, finally settling the long-standing dispute.

The way was then clear for negotiating a trade pact that would grant each country most-favored-nation status, permitting businessmen to establish offices in each country, providing reciprocal protection for patents, trade marks, and copyrights, as well as enabling regulated banking transactions. Each of these issues required detailed discussion, and it was only on the last day of Kreps' visit that an agreement was reached and initialed.

Two months later the trade agreement was signed, but Congressional approval was delayed due partly to a fear of an influx of Chinese textiles. To soothe Chinese irritation, Carter dispatched Vice-President Walter Mondale to China on a mission of explanation and goodwill.

Mondale in China

Mondale and his family visited China for eight days in August 1979 to reassure the Chinese of American friendship and to explain the delay in approving the trade agreement as due to a "logjam of congressional legislation." Mondale declared at the welcoming banquet: "If we strengthen our bilateral ties, we can both make dramatic economic progress, we can both enrich our cultures. . . . But above all . . . an enduring Sino-American relation will promote the stable international environment we both need to meet our domestic challenge and address problems of global concern."

In a major speech delivered at Beijing University and broadcast by the national Chinese television and radio networks, Mondale warned the Soviets and reassured China: "Any nation which seeks to weaken or isolate you in world affairs assumes a stance counter to American interests." He called for the withdrawal of Vietnamese troops from Cambodia and for an end to Vietnam's expulsion of its citizens as refugees—both declared prerequisites for American recognition of Vietnam.

Predictably pleased by Mondale's tone, what cheered the Chinese most were his assurances that the Carter administration would send the trade agreement to Congress by the end of the year before the Soviets could qualify for most-favored-nation status and that the United States would send experts to help build China's power dams while providing $2 billion in credit over a five-year period.

During the visit, Mondale signed two important agreements: a cultural exchange pact calling for the mutual reception of cinema and art delegations, film festivals, educational and athletic exchanges, as well as a visit to the United States by a Chinese delegation under Cultural Minister Huang Zhen; and an energy pact providing American assistance to China in developing twenty hydroelectric power stations, which required the cooperation of the Department of Energy, the

Tennessee Valley Authority, and the United States Army Corps of Engineers.

In all, Mondale's visit was a productive one, and it was to the Americans' credit that they pursued normalization through hard times with the diligence and attention it deserved. Mondale's mission breathed new life into the delicately unfolding relations between the two countries. A few months later, Carter, as promised, submitted the trade agreement for congressional approval. On January 24, 1980, congressional ratification was obtained.

Final Agreements

On September 17, 1980, Chinese Vice-Premier and veteran economic expert Bo Ibo signed four agreements with President Carter in Washington. They related to the exchange of direct airline service, access to ports, the establishment of new consulates, and limited growth in Chinese textile exports to the United States.

Pan-American Airlines had long desired routes to China, but Beijing would not grant permission until the Chinese Civil Aviation Administration received similar rights in the United States. Until the settlement of the claims dispute, Chinese airplanes ran the risk of detention at American airports because any American claimant could sue and attach Chinese property that entered the United States. Now, with the new agreement, the two countries could formally initiate scheduled airline service for the first time in thirty years. Each country designated an airline to operate two round trips each week on a route including New York, San Francisco, Los Angeles, Honolulu, Tokyo, Shanghai, and Beijing, with a second airline to be added by each in two years.

The marine agreement permitted each nation to call at designated ports (fifty-five American and twenty Chinese) and specified evenly divided cargo ratios: one-third in Chinese ships, one-third in American ships, and one-third in ships of other nationalities. The consular treaty, subject to confirmation by the Senate, allowed China to open three new consulates

(New York, Chicago, and Honolulu) and the United States also three more in China. It provided ground rules for the consulates and protection for the citizens of each country.

The textile agreement allowed Chinese exports to the United States to grow (3–4 percent each year for three years) above the unilateral quota set up by the United States in May 1979. It covered six categories of cotton garments and synthetic sweaters but not cloth. The new pact would raise the current level of American textile imports from China (7.2 percent) to one comparable to those of Hong Kong, Taiwan, South Korea, and Japan.

With the signing of these agreements, the long process of normalization which began in December 1978 was finally complete. Official Chinese-American relations reached a state of normalcy close to the pre-1949 level, Renewed diplomacy and trade symbolized American support of a modern, secure, and outward-looking China. Moreover, the United States was prepared to offer for sale to China high technology that had potential military implications.

Brown's Visit

In January 1980 Secretary of Defense Harold Brown went to China for a nine-day visit. Although the trip was arranged before Mondale's mission, it occurred at the time of the Soviet invasion of Afghanistan and hence took on added military significance. In Beijing, Brown seemed more eager than his hosts to develop some kind of security relationship in the face of the Soviet threat. At a banquet on January 6, he openly accused Moscow of overthrowing a friendly government in Afghanistan and executing its president and his family. Brown declared that Sino-American defense cooperation "should remind others that if they threaten the *shared interests* of the United States and China, we can respond with *complementary actions* in the field of defense as well as diplomacy."[35] Brown and Deng got along famously in their mutual mistrust of the Soviets. When Brown suggested that the two countries should coordinate their policies in the face of the Soviet threat, Deng went further proposing a world alliance to block Russian expansion.

As head of the American defense establishment, Brown was expected to offer China some military technology. The United States had stated repeatedly that it would not sell arms to China, but it had indicated a willingness to sell high-technology of dual application (civilian and military)—indeed, all technology at some point has military implications. Brown agreed to furnish China with a receiving station for data transmitted by the Landsat-D satellite, which can gather information about crops, oil, gas, and mineral exploration, and, of course, military information from space. In addition, the United States agreed to provide China with powerful computers for oil exploration. Obviously, the Carter administration had decided to quicken and to expand the transfer of high-technology equipment and skills to China.

To assess China's military capability and the state of its technology, Brown inspected the sixth tank division outside Beijing and watched an air show which featured the famous 38th Air Force Division. Four jets climbed steeply into the sky and then swooped down from a strafing run against dummy targets, showing considerable professional skill but also the limitations of the dated aircraft, copies of the MIG 19.

The Chinese air force reflected the military technology of the 1950s, as did the submarine and shipyard which Brown inspected in Wuhan. But in a few isolated areas Chinese achievements were quite advanced. The highly secret intercontinental missile, CSS-X-4, with a range of 6,000 miles (Beijing to Moscow or the United States' west coast) was not shown to Brown. In May 1980 it was tested successfully with two flights from western China to the Pacific.

China's limited capacity to pay for, as well as to absorb, high technology made for cautious selectivity in buying foreign hardware. Fearful of being overly dependent on one nation, the Chinese spread their purchases among several nations, including Britain, France, and West Germany, as well as the United States.

While military modernization was one of the Four Modernizations, and while the Chinese brass craved a technological revolution in the military, finance limited what could be acquired. The Third Plenum of the Fifth National People's Congress (September 1980) cut the military budget in the larger interests of economic rehabilitation, and only a modest program of acquiring sophisticated weapons and technology could be pursued.

However, if the American "tilt" toward China continues, a closer Sino-American military relationship may be accommodated. Several highly secret "contingency" studies have been made in the United States including the L-32 and Consolidated Guidance No. 8 which projected the emergency stationing of American warplanes in China and the arming of the Chinese at a total cost of $50 billion.[36]

Arms Sales

Sino-American relations took on a new dimension with the Reagan administration's decision to reverse the policy of refusing to sell arms to China. The decision was a result of a critical reassessment of the global strategic position of the United States and a pragmatic recognition that the United States cannot stand alone but needs the cooperation of China, Japan, and Europe in order to check the Soviet expansion. In a demonstration of anti-Soviet resolve, President Reagan dispatched Secretary of State Alexander Haig to China in June 1981 to discuss possible military coordination and to offer arms for sale on a case-by-case basis pending Congressional approval and consultation with American allies. The Chinese were gratified to find that Haig shared their perception of the Soviets: attempts at arms control and détente with the USSR were both disagreeable and futile.

At present, the decision on arms sales has greater political than military significance, for it restores the momentum in Sino-American relations and strengthens Washington's anti-Soviet stance. The Chinese are hardly able to purchase large quantities of expensive arms; they seem to be more interested in acquiring the technology to make the weapons themselves.

A Sino-American military relationship will develop slowly and cautiously at first, but when credits are made available to China later it may quicken into a quasi-alliance. China is already performing valuable services by pinning down a quarter of the Soviet forces on the Siberian border and by contributing to a general stability in the Asia-Pacific area. In addition, it seems that some secret American-Chinese military cooperation has already been in motion since the 1980 construction of two spy stations in northwest China. The stations utilize sophisticated American equipment to electronically monitor Soviet missile tests and other military activities, as well as to gather intelligence data. These stations have replaced those the United States lost in Northern Iran after the collapse of the Shah's government. Perhaps more importantly, a closer tie with China gives the United States the psychological security of having one billion people on its side, while China gains a strengthened shield against Soviet attack. As long as Chinese and American interests vis-à-vis the Soviet Union ccontinue to coincide, a deepening military relationship appears to benefit both nations.

It is impossible to sum up the vast benefits of normalization so soon—they continue ad infinitum, depending on one's interests and political persuasion. There are, however, benefits so basic that they are equally appreciated by all. First and foremost, a stable China is in the best interests of the United States and of world peace. In spite of great concern for Taiwan's security, the island after normalization appears to be in no great danger of a forceful takeover than before the mainland was recognized. China's repeated calls for the unification of Taiwan with the mainland have reduced the frenzied tension many felt. The expansion of cultural ties enables China to carefully choose the models for and means of modernization while opening wide the vast store of Chinese wisdom, skills, and arts, both traditional and modern, to an interested and appreciative America. Improved accessibility to advancements in Western technology and science will ease China's "New Long March" toward the Four Modernizations, while the expanding, if limited, market for American goods comes at a time when the United States needs to increase its exports. And finally, a well-equipped Chinese military may well safeguard what remains of Asian peace, while the Sino-American connection spells relief for the world from the vacillations of the Soviet-American polarity, with a new, more balanced triangle of power.

NOTES

1. Warren I. Cohen, *America's Response to China: An Interpretative History of Sino-American Relations,* 2nd ed. (New York, 1980), p. 244.
2. *The New York Times,* Dec. 15, 1978, p. 8.
3. *The Wall Street Journal,* Aug. 23, 1977.
4. According to Vice-Premier Deng Xiaoping, *The Christian Science Monitor,* Sept. 8, 1977, p. 3.
5. *The New York Times,* May 21 and 24, 1978.
6. *The Christian Science Monitor,* May 24, 1978.
7. Martin Tolchin, "How China and the U.S. Toppled Barriers to Normalization," *The New York Times,* Dec. 18, 1978, p. A12.
8. Chen Yisong.
9. *The Christian Science Monitor,* May 31, 1978.
10. Tolchin, p. A12.
11. Fox Butterfield, "After Camp David, Carter Set a Date for China Ties," *The New York Times,* Dec. 18, 1978, p. A12.
12. *Ibid.*
13. Takashi Oka, "Leonard Woodcock in China: Listening to the Unspoken," *The Christian Science Monitor,* April 2, 1980, p. B11.
14. *Ibid.*
15. Throughout the secret negotiations only five people in Washington, D.C., knew about them: Carter, Vance, Brzezinski, Defense Secretary Harold Brown, and Hamilton Jordan, the president's de facto chief-of-staff and top political advisor. In the Beijing American Liaison Office, only Woodcock and one other knew about them. The Washington group, however, was supported by Richard Holbrook, Assistant Secretary of State for East Asia and Pacific Affairs, Michel Oksenberg, National Security Specialist in the Far East, and Herbert J. Hansell, a State Department legal advisor.
16. The Gallop poll showed 58 percent approved the President's

action and 24 percent disapproved, with 18 percent no opinion. *The New York Times,* Jan. 14, 1979.

17. Stanley D. Bachrack, "The Death Rattle of the China Lobby," *Los Angeles Times,* Dec. 20, 1978.

18. The Department of State, Selected Documents No. 9: *U.S. Policy Toward China, July 15, 1971–January 15, 1979,* Office of Public Communication, Jan. 1979, pp. 45–46.

19. *Ibid.,* p. 48.

20. Linda Mathews, "Is the U.S. About to Take a Dragon by the Tail?" *Los Angeles Times,* Feb. 11, 1979.

21. *Los Angeles Times,* Dec. 26, 1978; *The Christian Science Monitor,* Dec. 18, 1978; *The New York Times,* Dec. 20, 1978.

22. Accompanied by legal advisor Herbert Hansell and Commander-in-Chief of U.S. Forces in the Pacific, Ad. Maurice Weisner.

23. *The New York Times,* Dec. 18, 1978, p. A10.

24. Ross Terrill, *The Future of China* (New York, 1978), p. 201.

25. Department of State News Release, Dec. 1978, "Diplomatic Relations with the People's Republic of China and Future Relations with Taiwan," Office of Public Communication, p. 3.

26. *The New York Times,* Dec. 17, 1978, p. 23.

27. *Los Angeles Times,* Dec. 25, 1978.

28. On October 17, 1979, U.S. District Court Judge Oliver Gasch ruled that President Carter acted unconstitutionally in terminating the pact: He must "receive the approval of two-thirds of the United States Senate or a majority of both houses of Congress . . . to be effective under our Constitution"; furthermore, the President could recommend treaty termination but the final decision could not be made by him alone. See *Los Angeles Times,* Oct. 20, 1979; *The Christian Science Monitor,* Nov. 14, 1979.

29. CBS radio broadcast by Marvin Kalb, Jan. 9, 1979.

30. *U.S. News & World Report,* Feb. 12, 1979, p. 26.

31. Marvin Stone, " 'No' to a China-U.S. Axis," *U.S. News & World Report,* Feb. 12, 1979, p. 88.

32. *Central Daily News,* Taipei, July 31 and Dec. 7, 1979; Oct. 15, 1981.

33. Lao Cai, Lai Chau, Cao Bang, and Mong Cai.

34. Anthony M. Soloman, "When 41¢ on the dollar is a good deal," *The Christian Science Monitor,* March 28, 1979. Mr. Soloman was Undersecretary for Monetary Affairs, U.S. Treasury. A similar settlement with the USSR was 12 cents on the dollar; with Hungary, 30 cents; with Poland and Rumania, 40 cents.

35. Italics added.

36. Jack Anderson, "U.S. 'Tilt' toward Peking Risks Soviet Reaction," *Santa Barbara News Press*, Sept. 28, 1980.

FURTHER READING

Alexiev, Alex, "Prospects for Accommodation," *Contemporary China*, III:2:36–46 (Summer 1979).

"An Interview with Teng Hsiao-p'ing: Calling for Stronger U.S.-China Ties and a United Front against Moscow," *Time* Magazine, Feb. 5, 1979, pp. 32–33.

Barnett, A. Doak, "Military-Security Relations between China and the United States," *Foreign Affairs*, LV:3:584–597 (April 1977).

Bellows, Thomas J., "Normalization: Process and Prognosis," *Sino-American Relations*, V:3:11–21 (Autumn 1979).

Butterfield, Fox, and William Safire, "China: Unraveling the New Mysteries," *The New York Times Magazine*, June 19, 1977, pp. 32–34, 48–59.

———, "After Camp David, Carter Set a Date for China Ties," *The New York Times*, Dec. 18, 1978, p. A12.

Chay, John (ed.), *The Problems and Prospects of American-East Asian Relations* (Boulder, 1977).

Ch'iu, Hungdah (ed.), *Normalizing Relations with the People's Republic of China: Problems, Analysis, and Documents*, (University of Maryland, School of Law, Occasional Papers, 1978).

Cohen, Jerome Alan, "A China Policy for the Next Administration," *Foreign Affairs*, LV:1:20–37 (Oct. 1976).

Cohen, Warren I., *America's Response to China: An Interpretative History of Sino-American Relations*, 2nd ed. (New York, 1980).

Copper, John Franklin, *China's Global Role* (Stanford, 1981).

Davies, John Paton, "America and East Asia," *Foreign Affairs*, LV:2:365–94 (Jan. 1977).

Department of State, "Diplomatic Relations with the People's Republic of China and Future Relations with Taiwan" (Washington, D.C., Dec. 1978).

———, *U.S. Policy Toward China, July 15, 1971–January 15, 1979*, Selected Documents No. 9, Office of Public Communication (Washington, D.C., 1979).

Folgel, Joshua A., and William T. Rowe (eds.), *Perspectives on a Changing China: Essays in Honor of Professor C. Martin Wilbur* (Boulder, 1979).

Garrett, Banning, "The China Card: To Play or Not to Play," *Contemporary China*, III:1:3–18 (Spring, 1979).

————, "Explosion in U.S.-China Trade?" *Contemporary China*, III:1:32–42 (Spring 1979).

Gurtov, Melvin, "China Invades Vietnam: An Assessment of Motives and Objectives," *Contemporary China*, III:4:3–9 (Winter 1979).

Harris, Lillian Craig, "Provocation and Polemic: Sino-Soviet Relations in 1978," *Contemporary China*, III:2:15–24 (Summer 1979).

————, "China and the Northern Tier: Shoring Up the Barrier to Soviet Southward Expansion," *Contemporary China*, III:4: 22–27 (Winter 1979).

Harrison, Selig S., *The Widening Gulf: Asian Nationalism and American Policy* (New York, 1978).

Johnson, Chalmers, "The New Thrust in China's Foreign Policy," *Foreign Affairs*, LVII:1:125–37 (Fall, 1978).

Karnow, Stanley, "East Asia in 1978: The Great Transformation," *Foreign Affairs*, LVII:3:589–612 (1979).

Kim, Samuel S., *China, the United Nations, and World Order* (Princeton, 1978).

Kim, Se-jin, "American Moral Psyche in Political Perspective," *Sino-American Relations*, VI:1:8–18 (Spring 1980).

Larkin, Bruce D., "China and Asia: The Year of the China-Vietnam War," *Current History*, 77:449:53–56, 83 (Sept. 1979).

Lieberthal, Kenneth, "The Foreign Policy Debate in Peking, as seen through Allegorical Articles, 1973–76," *The China Quarterly*, 71:528–54 (Sept. 1977).

Luttwak, Edward N., "Against the China Card," *Contemporary China*, III:1:19–31 (Spring 1979).

Martin, Edwin W., *Southeast Asia and China: The End of Containment* (Boulder, 1977).

Mendl, Wolf, *Issues in Japan's China Policy* (London, 1978).

Middleton, Drew, *The Duel of the Giants: China and Russia in Asia* (New York, 1978).

Nagorski, Andrew, "East Asia in 1980," *Foreign Affairs*, LIX:3: 667–95 (1980).

Nathan, Andrew J., "Prospects for Sino-American Relations and the Effects on Korea," *Contemporary China*, II:4:14–22 (Winter 1978).

Okita, Saburo, "Japan, China and the United States: Economic Relations & Prospects," *Foreign Affairs*, LVII:5:1090–1110 (Summer 1979).

Oksenberg, Michel, "China Policy for the 1980s," *Foreign Affairs*, LIX:2:304–22 (Winter 1980/81).

————, and Robert B. Oxnam, *Dragon and Eagle: United States-China Relations: Past and Future* (New York, 1978).

Rothenberg, Morris, "The Kremlin Looks at China," *Contemporary China*, III:2:25–35 (Summer 1979).

Scalapino, Robert A., "Asia at the End of the 1970s," *Foreign Affairs*, LVIII:3:693–737 (1979).

———, "Chinese Foreign Policy in 1979," in Robert B. Oxnam and Richard C. Bush (eds.), *China Briefing, 1980* (Boulder, 1980), pp. 75–85.

Segal, Gerald, "China and the Great Power Triangle," *The China Quarterly*, 83:490–509 (Sept. 1980).

Solomon, Richard H., "Thinking Through the China Problem," *Foreign Affairs*, LVI:2:324–56 (Jan. 1978).

Stuart, Douglas T., and William T. Tow (eds.), *China, The Soviet Union, and the West: Strategic and Political Dimensions for the 1980s* (Boulder, 1981).

Sutter, Robert G., *Chinese Foreign Policy after the Cultural Revolution, 1966–1977* (Boulder, 1978).

———, *China-Watch: Towards Sino-American Reconciliation* (New York, 1978).

Terrill, Ross, "China and the World: Self-Reliance or Independence," *Foreign Affairs*, LV:2:295–305 (Jan. 1977).

——— (ed.), *The China Difference* (New York, 1979).

———, "China in the 1980s," *Foreign Affairs*, LVIII:4:920–35 (Spring 1980).

Tretiak, Daniel, "China's Vietnam War and Its Consequences," *The China Quarterly*, 80:740–67 (Dec. 1979).

Yu, George T. (ed.), *Intra-Asian International Relations* (Boulder, 1978).

4

The Four Modernizations

If there is such a thing as a national consensus in China, it focuses on the commitment to the Four Modernizations—of agriculture, industry, science and technology, and national defense. The avowed goal is to turn China into a leading modern state by the year 2000. The Four Modernizations have been written into the party constitution (Eleventh Congress, August 18, 1977) and the state constitution (Fifth National People's Congress, March 5, 1978); hence the program should not be affected by changes in leadership. Yet, while modernization is the "general mission of a new historical period," an objective shared by Deng, Hua, Ye, and other leaders of both party and state, questions concerning its scope, timetable, and practical implementation are causing much heated debate.[1]

Zhou Enlai is generally credited with initiating the idea of the Four Modernizations in a report to the Fourth National People's Congress in January 1975. Actually, industrialization as the foundation of socialism is a Leninist principle which the Chinese Communists implemented as soon as they achieved power: more than one-half of China's total investment in the 1950s was allocated to industrial development. In 1963 Mao called for the "building of a modernized socialist power"; and it was in response to this call that Zhou proposed, at the Third National People's Congress, December 1964, the socialist construction of a "modernized agriculture, industry, national defense, and science and technology" to be accomplished "within a not too long period of history."[2] However, no concrete action followed due to the onset of the Cultural Revolution.

In January 1975, Zhou renewed his call for an "independent and relatively comprehensive industrial and economic system" by 1980, and an overall modernization of the four sectors before the end of the century. This speech, Zhou's last before a national congress, is generally considered the basis of the current Four Modernizations. Again, little came from it due to the obstruction of the Gang of Four, which condemned modernization as a "road to capitalist restoration." Too sick to fight, Zhou did not risk a confrontation with Mao's wife.

Zhou's chief ally, Deng Xiaoping, was not one to yield easily, however. In the fall of 1975 he drafted three key documents which later served as blueprints for the Four Modernizations.[3] These works were branded by the Gang as "Three Poisonous Weeds," and Deng became the prime target of the "Antirightist Deviationist Wind" Campaign. Deng fought a losing battle as long as the Gang had Mao's support; in his 1976 New Year's Message, Mao warned the nation against overemphasizing material progress.[4] Deng dropped out of sight after delivering Zhou's eulogy on January 15, 1976, and was dismissed from all posts after the Tian An Men Incident in April.

Not until the smashing of the Gang in October were the Four Modernizations revived. Chairman Hua seized the opportunity to promote them in a spirit of revolutionary vigor but without much economic expertise. In the months that followed (as Deng's rehabilitation was being negotiated), acceleration of the Four Modernizations was approved. In May 1977, at the "Learn from Daqing for Industry National Conference," veteran party economist Yu Qiuli declared:

Within the decade (1976–1985) we shall first erect a comparatively complete independent industrial system covering the entire country and accomplish fundamental technical renovation of the national economy. From this foothold we shall establish, step by step, six economic systems of different levels, in the Northeast, Northwest, and Southwest, and in North China, East China, and South Central China. Each shall have its unique features, be capable of independent operation, and exert maximum efforts for the development of agriculture, light industry and heavy industry.[5]

After Deng was formally reinstated, he delivered the closing address at the Eleventh Party Congress in August 1977, stressing the primacy of modernization. To promote the cause, a National Science Conference and a Military Political Work Conference was called in the following spring. At these meetings increasing differences of opinion were revealed between Hua and Deng; the former stressed the use of revolutionary spirit to guide modernization, while the latter emphasized hard work and detailed planning within accepted economic laws.[6] Nonetheless, the two shared a final vision of "electricity in rural areas, industrial automation, a new economic outlook, and greatly enhanced defense strength" by the close of the century.[7]

THE TEN-YEAR PLAN

At the first session of the Fifth National People's Congress in February 1978, Chairman Hua unveiled a grandiose ten-year modernization program for 1976–85; as two years had already passed, it was actually an eight-year plan. It detailed the major goals to be achieved in the four sectors.

The Industrial Sector

Investment for capital construction in industry was to equal or surpass that of the entire previous twenty-eight years, which was estimated at US$400 billion, and the annual rate of industrial growth was set at 10 percent. Hua called for the completion of 120 major projects, including: 10 iron and steel complexes, 10 oil and gas fields, 30 power stations, 8 coal mines, 9 nonferrous metal complexes, 7 major trunk railways, and 5 key harbors. It was hoped that by the end of the century Chinese industrial output in the major sectors would "approach, equal, or outstrip that of the most developed capitalist countries."[8]

Steel. In 1952 steel production (1.35 million tons) had already surpassed the pre-Liberation peak, and it rose to 18.67 million tons by 1960. The Great Leap cut the output back to 8 million tons in 1961, and the Cultural Revolution provided further inhibitions. It was not until 1970 that steel production recovered, reaching 25.5 million tons by 1973. Yet production decreased again under the Gang of Four—in 1976 only 21 million tons were produced. In short, from 1960 to 1976, only small gains were achieved.

The Ten-Year Plan called for increased production to 60 million tons by 1985 and 180 million tons by 1999. To achieve such major increases, a giant steel complex at Jidong (eastern Hebei), capable of producing 10 million tons a year, was planned under contract with German firms at a cost of $14 billion; a six-million-ton complex was to be constructed at Baoshan (a suburb of Shanghai) under contracts with Japanese firms with an estimated initial cost of $2 billion. A number of other sizable plants were to be built elsewhere, and existing plants were to be renovated.

Oil. Before 1957 China's petroleum production was insignificant (1.46 million tons of crude oil per year). Vast advances were made in the 1960s, with new discoveries and the establishment of the Daqing Oil Field in Manchuria, the Shengli Oil Field in Shantong province and the Dakang Oil Field in the Tianjin harbor area. Crude output doubled between 1960 and 1965 and again by 1969. By 1978 it had reached 104 million tons. The Ten-Year Plan called for the construction of ten new oil and gas fields costing $60 billion.[9]

Coal. Coal provides 70 percent of China's primary energy supply, but most of the mines are small and antiquated. The Ten-Year Plan called for eight new mines along with the renovation of existing ones in hopes of doubling production to 900 million tons a year. This means an annual growth rate of about 7.2 percent compared with 6.3 percent in 1970–77.

Electric Power. Surprisingly, the production of electricity is the weakest link in the modernization plan. In 1978 production totaled 256.6 billion kilowatt hours, ranking China ninth in the world in electricity production, but per capita consumption remained extremely low below both India and Pakistan. The Ten-Year Plan called for the construction of thirty power stations, twenty of them to be hydropower. The largest projects include the 2.7 million kilowatt Gezhouba hydropower station on the Yangtze River near Yichang (Hubei) and the 1.6 million kilowatt Longyang Gorge station on the upper reaches of the Yellow River near Sining (Qinghai). The thirty new plants will increase production by 6 to 8 million kilowatts per year—far short of the 13–14 percent growth rate needed to sustain the goal of a 10 percent annual increase in industry, and leaving nothing with which to increase personal consumption.

The Agricultural Sector

Agriculture is the foundation of the Chinese economy. It supplies 70 percent of the country's industrial raw materials, 60 percent of its total exports, and 80 percent of its domestic consumer goods.[10] Yet, since 1949, agriculture has consistently received less investment than industry and defense. Collectivization and the commune did not materially raise agricultural production. The 1963 movement "In agriculture, learn from Dazhai" was nothing more than a propaganda gimmick, and the Cultural Revolution drove agriculture to the brink of bankruptcy. On August 8, 1977, *Renmin Ribao* [People's daily] frankly stated that "whenever farms are hit by disastrous natural calamities, drastic reduction in output resulted; in the event of smaller disaster, smaller reduction; even with perfect weather conditions there was not much increase."[11] A Chinese leader admitted that "in 1977, the average amount of grain per capita in the nation was the same as the 1955 level; in other words, the growth of grain production was only about equal to the population growth plus the increase in grain requirements for industrial and other uses."[12] In October 1978 Deng remarked that "only through an all-out effort to restore agriculture to normalcy and increase production quickly can the entire economy be assured of fast development." Agricultural modernization is vital to the success of the Four Modernizations.

When he announced the Ten-Year Plan, Hua called for maximizing farm production through mechanization, electrification, irrigation, and higher utilization of chemical fertilizers. Specifically, the targets included:

1. Increase of gross agricultural products by 4–5 percent annually.
2. Increase of food output to 400 million tons by 1985 (from 285 million tons in 1977, a 4.4 percent annual growth).
3. Mechanization of 85 percent of major farming tasks.
4. Expansion of water works to assure one good *mou* (one-sixth acre) of dependably irrigated land per farming capita totalling 800 million *mou* (121 million acres).
5. Establishment of twelve commodity and food base areas throughout the nation.

Some estimated that the plan's agricultural modernization would require: (1) 12 million 15-horsepower tractors; (2) 4 million powered farm tools; (3) irrigation and pumping facilities totalling 40 million horsepower; (4) 320,000 combines; (5) 400,000 trucks and power machines; (6) 8 billion kilowatt hours of electricity; and (7) 66 million tons of chemical fertilizers.[13]

Such a vast undertaking would cost an estimated $33 billion. It would also require 2 million agricultural engineers and technicians, including 1.2 million mechanics to maintain tractors, combines, power tools and machines, 4 million to man pumping equipment, and 8 million truck drivers and farm products processing personnel. On the other hand, this mechanization of farm operations would release 100 million agricultural laborers to other lines of work. Relocating them and creating new job opportunities would cost $50 billion.[14] William Hinton, an American farm expert, questions the wisdom of fast mechanization in China in view of the abundance of labor.[15]

To bolster the slow agricultural growth rate of 2 percent annually since 1957, the government laid down several new guidelines. The "production team," hitherto the basic accounting unit responsible for any surplus or deficit, was replaced by the larger "production brigade." Next, the principle "to each according to his work " was adopted to stimulate farm initiative and enthusiasm; hence "more pay for more work and less pay for less work" has become a basic rural economic policy. In addition, encouragement of household "sideline production" should work to supplement the larger economy. Rural families do not own the communally distributed "private" plots but have the right to farm them. They cannot rent, sell, or transfer the land, but they do own its products. "Sideline" production makes up some 25 percent of total agricultural and subsidiary production. Finally, it is hoped that through intensive development, commune- and brigade-operated enterprises will be able to support large industries and the export trade.

With 800 million people working on farms, it is imperative to resolve the manifold agricultural problems and thus loosen the bottle-neck in China's economic development. Only so can the Four Modernizations expect to succeed.

Scientific Modernization

Science and technology are considered basic to successful modernization of the other three sectors. At the National Science Conference in March 1978, a Draft Outline National Plan for the Development of Science and Technology was presented by Vice-Premier Fang Yi, calling for: (1) achieving or approaching the 1970 scientific levels of advanced nations in various scientific and technological fields; (2) increasing professional scientific researchers to 800,000; (3) developing up-to-date centers for scientific experiments; and (4) completing a nationwide system of scientific and technological research. The Outline identified 108 items in twenty-seven fields as key projects for research.[16] It is hoped that by 1985 China would be only ten years behind the most advanced nations, with a solid foundation for catching up to or even surpassing the advanced nations by the end of the century.

To promote science and technology, the National Science and Technology Commission, inactive during the decade of the Cultural Revolution, was reactivated to formulate short-range (three-year), medium-range (eight-year), and long-range (to the year 2000) projects. Hua called for a "March on the Road of Science and Technology," and Deng personally appeared at the National Science Conference to set the tone for the new scientific attitude. Deng brushed aside the Maoist disdain for intellectuals and the "antirightist" bias; expertise is now preferred to "redness," and foreign-trained intellectuals, humiliated in the past, are now treated as cherished patriots and as part of the proletariat. A new respect for their knowledge has led to their reinstallment in important positions in universities and research organizations, and the younger and talented scientists and engineers are sent abroad for further studies. These intellectuals serve as China's bridge with foreign scientific circles.

Military Modernization

China has the largest regular armed force in the world, numbering some 4,325,000. The army alone includes 3,250,000 troops, and China's naval and air forces rank third internationally in terms of numbers.[17] But, except for pockets of intensive development in the strategic sector (e.g. nuclear bombs and ballistic missiles), Chinese military technology remains some twenty to thirty years behind the West. Troops are well trained, highly motivated, and politically indoctrinated but equipped with woefully inadequate weapons. The situation, brought about by a lack of funds and by an underdeveloped technology, worsened with Mao's emphasis on spirit over weapons. His idea of "people's war," employing large numbers of politically motivated, well-trained guerrillas to harass and drive out the invader is primarily a defensive notion, lacking offensive punch. The unspectacular Chinese invasion of Vietnam in 1979 clearly illustrates this. Su Yu, a brilliant strategist and former chief-of-staff, stated that Mao's concepts had "seriously shackled the people's minds and obstructed the development of military ideas."[18]

With extensive Soviet aid in the 1950s, the Chinese built up a nearly self-sufficient defense-manufacturing industry, and some of their products (e.g. the AK-47 rifle) rank among the world's best.[19] Yet, by and large, Chinese military technology is two or three decades out of date. Truly swift modernization would require massive purchases of foreign weapons and instruments; but that would be prohibitively expensive and also place China at the mercy of foreign suppliers. As the paramount consideration in China's long-term military planning is still the indigenous control of production capabilities, only selective purchases of high-technology systems and weaponry with special contracts for production in China are planned. The purchase of fifty British supersonic Spey jet engines, with plans for the engines to be manufactured in China with the assistance of Rolls Royce, and the purchase of several thousand HOT antitank missiles from France, with similar production agreements, are examples of this cautious selectivity.[20]

Yet problems still exist—after the purchase of the Spey engine technology, Chinese metallurgical capabilities were found insufficient to produce the alloys needed for the engines.[21] In addition, both the Spey engines and the HOT missiles are products of an already outmoded technology of the 1960s. Even the vertical take-off *Harrier* purchased from Britain has a short-range, a low-speed, and a high accident rate that reflects the technology of a decade past.[22] While acquiring such equipment may prevent the technological gap from widening, "stop-gap" measures will not ensure the achievement of China's modernization goals.

Chinese experts have visited advanced military establishments in the West to witness the state-of-the-art military technology rather than to purchase it—China's defense needs are so vast and diverse as to defy the country's ability to pay for them. Still, the military seeks to prepare the country for a "people's war under modern conditions" requiring "automatic computerized countdown, improved communications and command systems, and rapid, motorized, transportation facilities," with conventional as well as strategic weapons.[23] Under increasing pressure from the brass, Chinese leadership is leaning toward a compromise: "Serious effort should be made to implement the policy of integrating military with non-military enterprises and peacetime production with preparedness against war, and fully tap the potential of the machine-building and national defense industries."[24]

Chinese leaders recognize the urgent need to update obsolete equipment on a massive scale but also see its astronomical cost. Although China's defense budget is a state secret, Western estimates put it at $32.8 billion in 1976, the third largest globally.[25] A British source put China's 1978 defense spending at 7–10 percent of the GNP, or about $35 billion.[26] The production of new equipment, spare parts, and maintenance account for 58 percent of that figure. To modernize fully even a portion of China's military would cost an impossible $300 billion by 1985.[27] Since such an expenditure would require massive infusions of foreign capital and equipment, military modernization occupies a low priority. While modernizing science and technology will eventually benefit the military, it is clear that military modernization will be a highly selective and slow process.

The ultimate irony may be that after straining to acquire current state-of-the-art technology and weaponry, it will take the Chinese five to ten years to integrate such modern equipment into existing structures. It would be imperative to upgrade research and development in laser, metallurgy, optics, communications, and computers; to prepare the scientific-managerial infrastructure for research, development, and production; as well as to train military personnel to use, maintain, repair, and refurbish the new equipment. By that time new strides will have been made in the more advanced countries, and China will yet remain behind by ten to fifteen years. While this would represent an improvement over present capabilities, it would have to be seen as falling short of true modernization goals.

MAJOR PROBLEMS OF MODERNIZATION: CAPITAL, MANPOWER, AND PLANNING

The most serious problems in China's modernization are the shortages of investment capital and of qualified personnel. Success of the Four Modernizations is dependent on the resolution of these two basic problems. The Ten-Year plan would cost somewhere between $350 billion and $630 billion;[28] China's gold and foreign exchange reserve (1978–79) was only $4.5 billion.[29] According to an American estimate, China's GNP in 1978 was $407 billion.[30] Assuming a 5.5 percent annual growth rate, the GNP for 1978–85 would generate $3,956 billion (in 1977 price); if 10 percent of this were allocated for developmental investment, China could conceivably raise $400 billion from domestic savings, still leaving the nation with a shortfall of more than $200 billion.[31]

Past practices may shed light on China's financial stringency. During 1949–59, industrial investment totaled $46.2 billion: $10 billion came from confiscated properties of landloards and capitalists, $3 billion from Soviet credits and loans, and the rest from the difference between the state's low-price purchases of farm products and its high-price sales of industrial products to the farm sector. Of course, the first two sources no longer exist and the third has been severely damaged by the Cultural Revolution and the Gang. Hua reported, "Between 1974 and 1976, the influence of the Gang of Four caused losses worth $63 billion in industrial output and $25 billion in state revenue."[32] The Gang severely crippled the economy, and the consequences have continued to plague the country. In September 1978, an estimated 25 percent of state enterprises were operating in the red.

To raise capital for modernization, China has resorted to clearly un-Maoist methods. First, tourism has been vastly expanded, and the "lure of Cathay" is proving both irresistible to foreigners and highly profitable to China. In 1978, 100,000 foreigners and 600,000 overseas Chinese visited China. Tourism generated $607.2 million in 1980. To attract more foreign visitors, new hotels are being built, increasing the present room capacity of 30,000 to 80,000 by 1985.[33]

Second, China has devised innovative cooperative investment projects with foreign firms. For instance, Konrad Hornschuch AG of West Germany agreed to build two petrochemical plants in China at $21 million, with 50 percent of the first five years' production as payment. The Japanese firm Itoman & Company contracted to provide materials, equipment, and advice to a Shanghai textile plant in exchange for the right to market its line of products.[34]

Third, China has adopted a more flexible attitude toward foreign loans. Formerly, Beijing rejected foreign loans out of fear of foreign control; if a loan was negotiated it was euphemistically referred to as "progress" or "deferred" payments. But on December 6, 1978, China openly concluded a loan agreement with a British consortium of ten banks for $1.2 billion at a 7.25 percent interest rate; by mid-April 1979 some $10 billion in foreign loans and credits had been negotiated.[35] Generally, however, the Chinese remain reluctant to accept large, long-term loans, due to their limited ability to repay and to their historically founded fear of foreign domination.

In spite of these fund-raising devices, China's capital remains very limited, severely constricting the potential for rapid, large-scale importation of foreign equipment and high technology. Indeed, every step in the modernization process raises the problem of insufficient funds.

The shortage of qualified manpower is an equally serious handicap in China's modernization drive limiting the country's capacity to absorb the new technology. Between 1949 and 1966, Chinese higher education produced 1.8 million university graduates of whom at least one-half majored in sciences and engineering.[36] But the twelve-year disruption of the Cultural Revolution caused a loss of 200,000 college graduates per year, a total of 2.4 million or at least 1.2 million scientists and engineers.[37] There is also an extreme shortage of scientific-managerial personnel capable of running large-scale modern industrial plants. Even skilled labor is in short supply. Of the country's 94 million-member work force, only 1.6 percent can be considered technical personnel, and 73 percent of the skilled labor force has received an education of only junior high or lower. This lack of training and education makes it difficult for workers to operate and maintain the sophisticated imported equipment and to use work manuals, many of which remain in foreign languages due to a lack of qualified translators. As a result, many expensive foreign machines are still unpacked in their original crates, or are left rusting in the open air.

The integration of Western science and technology into Chinese society is a century-old problem; China's present predicament is clearly the result of the failure to integrate science with the larger society. China's oldest well-educated group, those scientists and intellectuals trained in the West and Japan from 1920 to 1949, were severely attacked during the Anti-rightist movement of 1957 and persecuted beyond human endurance during the Cultural Revolution. They were despised, ridiculed, and derided as the "stinking No. 9's," ranking behind landlords, the rich, counterrevolutionaries, bad elements, rightists, rebels, special agents, and capitalist roaders. Many were plagued and harassed to death, or driven to suicide; others were jailed, tortured, maimed, and crippled. In 1973 an American estimate put qualified Chinese scientific and technological personnel at an incredibly small 65,000, while a leading Chinese scientist and educator[38] gave an even more alarming figure of 60,000 in 1978.[39]

However, with the reopening of the universities and with admissions once again based on a strictly administered national examination, Chinese higher education is recovering and promises to produce a new generation of well-educated intellectuals. The government has designated eighty-eight "key" universities and restored dismissed professors to responsible positions. Academic subjects are receiving new respect, and students study diligently in hopes of further education abroad. By 1981 more than 5,000 qualified graduate and senior scholars were abroad for advanced research and study, and about 130 delegations visited the United States monthly. The academic atmosphere is improving in the universities; but many intellectuals, recently released from the so-called "cow shed" (*niu-lan*), understandably feel insecure and are timid, fearful of speaking their minds, and unwilling to commit their views to writing. To arouse their enthusiasm will require a long period of reassurance and trust. Yet most agree that China's academic institutions are now freer than at any time in the past thirty years.

To further cultivate scientifically oriented personnel, the government restored the Chinese Academy of Sciences to a position of power and honor. High-quality basic research is encouraged, and five-sixth of the scientist's time is devoted to scientific work. Scientists and other intellectuals are encouraged by the fact that their work is no longer evaluated by political criteria. In addition to new opportunities to study abroad, famous foreign scholars are being invited to give lectures; and training is now available in scientific management, operations research, and systems analysis.

While these undertakings are worthy remedies to past malpractices, it takes time to train the personnel necessary to run a modern economy—it is not a process which can be rushed. Today, China may have 400,000 college-educated scientists and engineers of varying competence, but middle-echelon technical personnel, skilled workers, and local administrators are in desperately short supply.[40] At the same time, it is difficult to work around the party cadres who are entrenched in both central and local scientific and research organizations. Threatened by the new primacy of scientific knowledge and expertise, they band together to protect their vested interests, inevitably slowing modernization.

Generally, Chinese scientific and technical personnel can be categorized into five groups. The first consists of those trained before Liberation in 1949, including many educated abroad. Formerly the target for attack, this small group now enjoys great prestige serving as China's scientific liaison with the outside world. The second group consists of those trained after Liberation in the Soviet Union (or by Russians in China) during the 1950s, who are now in middle-echelon positions. The third consists of college graduates of the period before the Cultural Revolution in 1966, now in their late thirties and early forties. Many of them have been sent abroad for further study and may prove a powerful force in the future. The fourth group is made up of students of worker, peasant, or soldier (*gong nong ping*) backgrounds trained during the Cultural Revolution. With the exception of a few, they have been inadequately prepared for the tasks of modernization. The fifth group is comprised of college students admitted to the universities after 1977 and represent in a real sense the future of Chinese scientific manpower. Until this last and growing group is fully trained, China's power to absorb the technology of modernization will remain very limited.

The current lack of qualified experts has led to a poor beginning of modernization projects. The most conspicuous case is the Baoshan steel complex near Shanghai. Originally it was to be a $2 billion complex with an annual production capacity of 6 million tons. Modeled after the highly modern and successful Japanese Kimitsu plant, a thousand Japanese experts and technicians came to help with its operation. Unfortunately, the site was ill-chosen, located on swampy land at the edge of the Yangtze River. Hundreds of thousands of steel pilings had to be driven into the ground before the physical structures of the complex could be built. When work began in late 1979, it was quickly discovered that the power supply was insufficient and that the site lacked accessible deep water ports to receive iron ore from Australia and Brazil. The first stage was competed only after confronting countless difficulties and spending $5 billion. The financial burdens were unbearable, and the Chinese government unilaterally halted the second stage of construction by the end of 1980 causing consternation and anger on the part of the Japanese suppliers.

Another giant steel complex, to be built wihh German aid in Jidong, Hebei (at $14 billion for a production capacity of 10 million tons per year), is located in an earthquake-prone region—its progress has been faltering at best. A third example of poor planning concerns the Wuhan Iron and Steel Company, which purchased West German equipment capable of producing 4 million tons of steel annually. The huge German machines required so much electricity that they drained the electricity supply of the entire province, making other industries inoperable. Furthermore, Wuhan has been unable to supply the six million tons of raw steel required to produce four million tons of finished steel per year. For each day production is delayed, an estimated two million German marks are lost—a deplorable waste in capital-scarce China.

RETRENCHMENT AND REVISED PRIORITIES

The original Ten-Year Plan was more of a political wish than an economic blueprint, and it lacked careful study as to its feasibility. During the first year of the program, some 100,000 construction projects were launched by the government costing $40 billion; with military and scientific procurements the total reached 24 percent of the 1978 national income of $198 billion. Large foreign contracts were also negotiated including the Baoshan steel complex ($2 billion), the Jidong steel complex ($14 billion), and a hotel construction project with the U.S. International Hotel Corporation ($500 million). In addition, regional organizations contracted a large number of sizable agreements with foreign suppliers, which, together with local construction projects, raised the total investment for 1978 to 36 percent of the national income, quite close to the 40 percent rate of the disastrous Great Leap years. Such zealous over-spending was clearly insupportable.[41]

Economic realities soon set in to force a critical reassessment. A debate at the highest level took place regarding the scope and priorities of investment. In July 1978, Hu Qiaomu, president of the Chinese Academy of Social Sciences, called for greater emphasis on agricultural production which reflected the results of the top echelon's reassessments.[42] Similar sentiments were expressed in December 1978 at the meetings of the Eleventh Central Committee (Third Plenum). On February 24, 1979, the *Renmin Ribao* [People's daily] editorialized against a hasty, impractical approach to modernization: "Judging from our experience . . . China has suffered more from rashness than from conservatism. . . . Many projects were started hurriedly without the preparatory work that should have been done, thus failing to proceed from realities. . . . A frightful waste of manpower and materials was involved in these projects."

China's limited financial and scientific resources forced leaders to reassess the Ten-Year Plan critically. It was decided that the top priority should be agriculture, the foundation of the economy, followed by light industry, which could meet domestic demands and earn foreign exchange, and then heavy industry. Capital investment in agriculture was increased from $26 billion (Ch$40 billion) to $59 billion (Ch$90 billion), and light and export industries also received new allocations. Within heavy industry, steel production targets were slashed from 60 million to 45 million tons; but coal, electric power, petroleum, and building industries retained priorities for investments.[43] Projects that could be completed quickly and earn foreign exchange were encouraged, and bank loans rather than government appropriations were planned for future investment projects. On the other hand, projects requiring huge amounts of capital and facing problems in resources, raw materials, location, transportation, technical capabilities, or energy supply were delayed or suspended.

At the Fifth National People's Congress (second session, June 1979). Hua Guofeng announced a three-year period

(1979–81) for the "adjustment, reconstruction, consolidation, and improvement" of the national economy. Blaming Lin Biao and the Gang of Four for sabotaging the economy, he ruefully admitted: "We had not taken this into full account, and some of the measures we adopted were not prudent enough."[44]

The immediate effect of the retrenchment was the halting of 348 important heavy industrial projects (including 38 steel and metallurgical plants) and 4,500 smaller ones. Capital investment for 1979 was reduced to 34.8 percent of state expenditures. Specifically, investments in the steel, machinery, and chemical industries were most deeply cut, losing from 30–45 percent of their investment allotment in 1979–80.[45] Construction also suffered, with a 33 percent cut in Shanghai and a 40 percent cut for Inner Mongolia. Simultaneously, investment in agriculture increased from 10.7 percent of the state budget in 1978 to 14 percent in 1979 and 16 percent in 1980, while in textile and light industries investment rose from 5.4 percent in 1978 to 5.8 percent in 1979 and perhaps 8 percent in 1980.

The retrenchment was necessitated not only by China's limited foreign credit, financial resources, and absorptive power but also by the unexpectedly high cost of invading Vietnam in 1979. In addition, original estimates of oil production and its export potential were far too optimistic, and disappointing performance in the energy sector dampened China's hope of using oil exports to finance modernization. The 1978 budgetary deficit was $6.5 billion and climbed to $11.3 billion in 1979.[46] Clearly, more sophisticated and thorough economic planning was required. Saburo Okita, chairman of the Japan Economic Research Center and an architect of the Japanese economic miracle, was invited to China as a consultant.

Rearranging developmental priorities served to correct many of the causes of structural disequilibrium in the Chinese economy: (1) the imbalances within fuel, power, and raw material industries; (2) the imbalance between light and heavy industries; (3) the imbalance between agriculture and industry; and (4) the imbalance between capital investment and consumption.

As a result of retrenchment, the new scaled-down targets for

1985 and the projected output of the five major industries by 1985 appear as follows:[47]

	1978	1979	1985 (Ten-Year Plan)	1985 (revised)	1985 (most likely output)
Steel (million tons)	31.8	34.5	60	45	42
Coal (million tons)	618	635	900	800	745
Crude Oil (million tons)	104	106.2	500	300	135
Electricity (billion kwh)	256.6	282	n.a.	n.a.	455
Cement (million tons)	65.2	73.9	100	100	90

Of note is the very small growth in coal and oil production, the two main energy sources. Coal output grew 12.3 percent in 1978 but only 2.75 percent in 1979. Crude oil registered a 1.9 percent increase in 1979 compared to 11 percent in 1978 and an annual 22.5 percent between 1957 and 1977. This vast decrease may suggest that oil output at current producing sites has already peaked, and thus indicate the necessity for new exploration. Electricity output also fell from an annual growth rate of 13 percent between 1957 and 1978 to 9.9 percent in 1979 and 2.9 percent in 1980.[48]

The overall view clearly shows that energy and transportation remain major obstacles in the modernization plan. Oil, coal, and electricity production fall far short of meeting new demands. While freight volume increased 9.7 times from 1950 to 1978, railway mileage increased only 1.4 times—transport lines are strained to the limit. Unless the energy and transportation bottlenecks are eased, China's modernization will be constrained. The small increase in oil output has drastically reduced China's ability to earn foreign currency to finance the purchase of foreign high technology.

It is possible that some additional income might be acquired from the textile and light industries which can more easily meet consumer demands and earn foreign exchange. As a result of increased state investment, bank loans, and better material, textile output rose 30 percent in the first quarter of 1980 over the same period in 1979, and light industry rose by 21 percent.[49] But it is questionable whether these sources will generate enough funds to hasten materially the date of modernization.

PROFIT, MATERIAL INCENTIVE, AND STRUCTURAL REORGANIZATION

It comes as an odd realization that everyone in socialist China today is interested in profit and openly talks about making more money. People who worked half-heartedly under Mao's regime are now enlivened by hopes of improving their lives through increased earnings. The new leadership has encouraged these hopes in the interest of increasing production. Indeed, the government has promoted workers' incentives and initiatives by giving material rewards, reforming the industrial organization, and appointing experts with proven managerial skills as plant directors. It is hoped that these reforms will increase the efficiency and output of existing plants as new ones will take time to build and contribute little to the economy for several years. Hua pointed out in 1979: "In the next eight years, and especially in the next three, our existing plants must be the foundation for the growth of production." China invited Western and Japanese firms to invest in renovating these plants, but most preferred to invest in new plans rather than to put money into obsolescent factories.

The government recognizes material reward as a powerful incentive for increased production. It was noted that during the First Five-Year Plan (1952–56) when wages rose 7.4 percent annually, productivity increased correspondingly with gross industrial production rising 18 percent per annum. During the Cultural Revolution the bonus system and wage increases were abolished, and the result was decreased production and increased absenteeism. In 1977, after more than a decade, a 10 percent wage increase was granted to 64 percent of the nonagricultural workers, and bonus and piece rate systems were restored in 1978.[50]

Toward industrial reorganization, farm machinery corporations were established in the Six Economic Regions to coordinate efforts at modernization and to reduce duplication and waste. Each province has a tractor motor company, an instruments and meter company, a ball bearing factory, and a machinery export company. To improve management, Maoist worker-participation-in-management and cadre-participation-in-labor schemes were rejected in favor of expert, professional management, with the hope of insuring efficiency and accountability. Economic norms were set up to measure an enterprise's output, including variety, quality, cost, profit, resource allocation, and productivity. Each enterprise has a fixed quota for output, personnel, materials, capital assets, and liquid capital; in return, the enterprise guarantees the quantity and quality of products, labor and production costs and expected state profit. Surpassing production quotas entitles the enterprise to a part of the profit. Thus profit and material reward are officially used as the means to raise production and efficiency.

In addition, the government is streamlining the industrial infrastructure as well as the management and control system. In the past, the system usually worked from the top down with an overconcentration of decision-making power at the central level causing duplication, waste, and a lack of initiative and enthusiasm among workers. In 1979 the government consolidated some 25,000 to 50,000 marginal enterprises into 970 specialized companies, each with decision-making powers to suit local requirements. Each is allowed to: (1) prepare production plans and sell above-quota products to other units; (2) keep 5 percent of profits on quota production and 20 percent on above-quota production; (3) reward more work with more pay and allow workers to control their own welfare and bonus funds; and (4) receive bank loans for investment.[51] In addition, five special economic regions have been established in

Beijing, Shanghai, Tianjin, Guangdong, and Fujian, with power to negotiate with foreign concerns and keep part of their foreign currency earnings.[52]

The new system, borrowing heavily from Yugoslavian and Romanian models, combines central planning with local initiative and market mechanisms to form a blend of capitalist and socialist structures. To say that capitalism has returned to China is an oversimplification; rather, some capitalist management techniques and an emphasis on profit margins have appeared in hopes that those enterprises operating in the red can be made profitable.

Although "private enterprise" has not returned, "individual economic undertakings" are on the rise. Thus, an energetic citizen called Yen converted a tea room into a booming Multi-Service Center selling 500 items and grossing $9 million a year. A Mrs. Liu, with the help of two sons, operates a family restaurant with such success that reservations have to be made days ahead, and waiting lines are a common scene. The economic atmosphere is also freer today than at any time in the past thirty years.

THE CONSEQUENCES OF RAPID MODERNIZATION

Just as there are problems in achieving modernization, there are also problems created by its accelerated achievement. First and foremost is inflation, which was almost nonexistent in earlier periods when the government deliberately adopted a policy of low wages and low commodity prices. When the people had little purchasing power, the demand for goods was kept low and prices were stable. With the increase in wages and government procurement prices for farm products (up 20–50 percent by 1977–79), the state correspondingly raised sale prices on various commodities creating inflation officially computed at 5.8 percent in 1979 but more likely reaching 15 percent. The upward spiral of price increases has continued unabated reaching an annual rate of 15–30 percent in 1980, while the light industry growth was only 9.7 percent. When prices increase faster than productivity, an inflationary psychology has set in, resulting in a black market and speculation. Government budgets also reveal growing deficits: $11.3 billion in 1979, $10–12 million in 1980, and perhaps $6 billion in 1981. To offset the deficits, the Ministry of Finance decided in the spring of 1981 to issue $3.3 billion in ten-year maturity bonds at 4 percent interest per annum. Government enterprises, administrative organizations, communes, and the army have been urged to buy according to their ability, but individuals seem free to purchase the bonds as they choose.[53] The floating of bonds indicates the financial difficulties China is facing.

Another immediate consequence of inflation and overzealous spending was the decision to cut back major construction projects by 40 percent in 1981. Many large projects involving foreign companies have been abruptly terminated. The Japanese, who entered the China market early, have fared the worst: total Japanese losses are estimated at $1.5 billion including the Baoshan steel complex and three petrochemical projects. The Germans fared less badly while the Americans, who entered the China market late, suffered the least. The Chinese simply explained that they could not afford to go ahead with these costly projects at this time and agreed to compensate for losses incurred without setting definite figures.[54] Foreigners understood China's financial dilemma but had to question the nation's international credibility when agreements entered into in good faith were unilaterally cancelled. There is no doubt that China's reputation as a reliable trader has been affected.

Cancellations of construction projects have led to the layoff of numerous workers, intensifying the already serious unemployment problem. China once boasted that its socialist system guaranteed employment for every able body, declaring proudly that there was no unemployment in China—there were only those awaiting job assignment! Semantics aside, overstaffing was common and a job requiring one was frequently shared by three at low wages. But construction cancellations and modernization of factories have demanded a reduction in personnel resulting in the loss of many jobs. While $10 billion has been invested in new foreign-style plants, relatively few new jobs have been created. Meanwhile, an estimated 10 to 15 million new workers enter the labor force annually. In the past, surplus manpower was forcibly dispersed to the countryside or hinterlands, but in the last three years this practice has been relaxed, and many who were previously so dispersed have managed to return to their home towns. About 80 percent of the over one million youths who were "sent downward" (*xia-fang*) from Shanghai have furtively returned. Although half of them have found some employment, others seem to have lost all hope. Unemployment in China is estimated at around 20 million in 1981.

Another anomalous phenomenon of modernization is the emergence of new classes in a so-called classless society. Modernization has given new prestige to the scientists, engineers, technicians, plant managers, writers, artists, and other intellectuals who will lead China's "Great Leap Outward." There is a new feeling that "among all activities, only science and technology are lofty." Scientists and intellectuals along with high party members now constitute a privileged upper class; urban workers of productive enterprises and lower echelon cadres form the second class, with farmers and those living in the countryside at the bottom of the totem pole. The selective sending of scholars and students abroad for advanced education, many of whom are blood relatives of high party members, further strengthens the elitist trend and widens the class cleavages.

Another deepening problem arises from the increasing disparity between the city and the countryside and among various industrial enterprises themselves. Since the government has opted for an "enclave" strategy of locating key industries in selected urban areas, these areas are more likely to enjoy the fruits of modernization—higher wages, greater upward mobility, and a higher standard of living. An average industrial worker in a city earns about $40 a month with an additional bonus, while the average monthly cash income of a peasant is only $5–7. It is not unusual for a city worker to earn six to eight times more than a peasant, and scientific or technical personnel over ten times more. Within the industrial sector, the profit is vastly uneven: in 1978 the oil industry enjoyed a 40 percent profit margin; electricity, 31 percent; metallurgy, 13 percent; and coal mining, only 1 percent. Since profit decides not only levels of investment but also the size of bonuses and fringe benefits, it deeply affects the worker's life style. Differences in rewards lead to different degrees of enthusiasm for work.

A further conflict exists between the production enterprises and the state commercial departments. In the past, vital materiel for enterprises was supplied by the Ministry of Material Allocation. Now each enterprise is allowed to sell some materials and products to consumers, competing with the government's commercial departments for profit. With the authorization to engage in foreign negotiations and trade, five provincial-municipal organizations set up offices in Hong Kong and Shanghai to sell their products directly to foreign trades, causing jealousy, competition, price wars, and confusion.

Beneath all the adverse consequences of rapid modernization lies what may be the most serious of China's problems—a crisis of confidence. After thirty years of socialist construction, the country remains poor and backward. Past reports of achievements have often been exposed as pure propaganda, and many, especially the young, have lost faith in the superiority of socialism. There is a conspicuous lack of confidence in achieving a true modernization. Young people are especially critical of the party cadres' privileged status and of bureaucratism, and on the basis of past performance doubt both their capability and sincerity in implementing modernization programs. Indeed, many middle- and lower-echelon party members in responsible positions but lacking scientific expertise are threatened by the new demands of modernization. They secretly resist, sabotage, and slow new undertakings which run counter to their interests.[55] There is now a popular saying: "The two ends are hot, but the middle is cold"—meaning the leaders and the people want modernization but the middle-level bureaucrats resist change. Chinese newspapers and journals openly discuss China's triple crises: a lack of faith, confidence, and trust in the party and the government.[56]

The original Ten-Year Plan is hardly mentioned now; even the three-year readjustment plan is heard of less and less. It appears that a new Ten-Year Plan based on economic realities and careful investigation is in the making for 1981–90. Its scope is no larger than the first plan's, but it gives the country five more years to achieve the original goals. With this breathing space, if the 1980 industrial and agricultural growth rate of 6 percent and 4 percent respectively can be maintained, by 1990 aggregate industrial production could conceivably increase by 80 percent, agricultural output by 50 percent, and per capita income by 66 percent from $266 to $400.[57]

FOREIGN VALUE AND CHINESE ESSENCE

Modernization has been a goal in China for more than a century. The late Qing court, the Nationalist government, and the Communist leadership all have tried to launch China on the road to modernization. Mao Zedong, in spite of his emphasis on peasants and grass root involvement, was an ardent supporter of industrialization though he knew little of economic planning. It was under Mao that China received from the Soviet Union the "most comprehensive technology transfer in modern history": 11,000 Russian experts worked in China during the 1950s and 15,000 Chinese were trained in the Soviet Union. China imported 157 complete plants from Russia and Eastern Europe representing 27 percent of total investment in machinery and equipment. The Sino-Soviet split in 1960 caused an abrupt termination of Soviet assistance, and during the Cultural Revolution other foreign technological and educational acquisition virtually ceased. While the alternative to Soviet and Eastern European aid was Western capitalist technology and equipment, learning from the West and Japan was considered highly dishonorable. In September 1975 a spokes-man for the Gang of Four proclaimed:

> Politically, "wholesale Westernization" meant loss of sover-eignty and national humiliation, a total sell-out of China's independence and self-determination. . . . Ideologically, "wholesale Westernization" was meant to praise what is foreign and belittle what is Chinese. . . . Economically, "wholesale Westernization" was aimed at spreading a blind faith in the Western capitalist material civilization so as to turn the Chinese economy into a complete appendage of imperialism.[58]

Thus the Maoists avocated self-reliance. Mao recognized China's backwardness as much as he was aware of its limited resources. He feared the effects of modernization on such sensi-tive issues as income distribution, worker status, and the revival of elitism and bureaucratism at the expense of egali-tarianism. Yet self-reliance and the rejection of foreign tech-nology for nearly two decades (1958–76) left China in an undeveloped abyss of poverty, while other countries through technological innovations charged ahead by leaps and bounds. Pragmatic leaders realized the dangers inherent in Mao's policy, but none dared oppose it.

With Mao's death and the demise of the Gang, the way has been cleared for a new start to make up for lost time. A crash program for modernization has been launched, with Hua in the lead and Deng as the main spirit of the New Leap Outward. They assume that science, technology, and the dy-namics of technological change are basically politically neutral and classless, and that they can be transplanted without injury to Chinese social and cultural institutions.[59] They have opted for a concentrated development of selected areas in key sectors of the Chinese economy through the imposition and internal development of science and technology. This "enclave" ap-proach will undoubtedly result in encapsulated regions of progress to the detriment of a more general technological as-similation.

In the zealous spirit of the post-Gang period, there seems to be an obsession with the notion that in little more than two decades, science can save China, rescue it from backwardness and poverty, and elevate it into the front ranks of the advanced states. The aim is worthy, but the grandiose targets and the stringent timetable seem unrealistic. High technology is extremely expensive, and its absorption and dissemination require both time and properly trained personnel. Problems with the industrial infrastructure, scientific management, specialization, standardization, and serialization were not considered in the original Ten-Year Plan. It will be years before scientific methods of operation and new techniques can filter down to the masses of workers, creating the necessary ability and enthusiasm for a national modernization drive.

Chinese leaders proclaim that they do not intend to ape the West but will forge a "Chinese-styled modernization." Yet the knowledge and skills associated with foreign technology will inevitably influence the thinking and behavior of those who acquired them. The late Qing debate on the "fundamentals versus application" (*tiyong*) dichotomy will reappear in a different form. Western scientists in China and "returned" students trained in advanced countries will undoubtedly exert new influences on Chinese life and thinking.

The cultural consequences of contact with foreign ideology, institutions, and ways of life cannot be totally contained, despite party admonitions and exhortations to the contrary. Hopefully, the Chinese will achieve a happy medium whereby they will indeed become modern in thought and in their specialties without sacrificing the distinctiveness of their Chinese origin. While the meeting of a particular timetable for China's modernization cannot be assured, the leadership's increasingly pragmatic goals do seem to point toward the eventuality of the successful modernization of the Chinese nation—perhaps thirty years into the next century.

NOTES

1. The Chinese government has never disclosed the complete blueprint of the Ten-Year Four Modernizations Plan. It is only from various reports on the work of the government, inter-

views, and scattered reports that we piece together the general outlines of the Plan.

2. Chao Yu-shen, "Chinese Communist Attempt to Modernize Industry," in *Chinese Communist Modernization Problems* (Taipei, 1979), pp. 29–30 (hereafter to be cited as *Modernization Problems*).

3. 1. "On General Guidelines of the Party's Nationwide Activities."
   2. "Summary Outlines of the Academy of Sciences' Activity Reports."
   3. "Certain Issues Concerning Accelerated Industrial Development."

4. *The New York Times,* Jan. 2, 1976, pp. 1, 4.

5. *Renmin Ribao* [People's daily], May 8, 1977. Tr. mine.

6. Li Tien-min, "Teng Hsiao-p'ing's Past and Future," in *Modernization Problems,* pp. 90–91.

7. Liu Keng-sheng, "Modernization of Peiping's Science and Technology," in *Modernization Problems,* p. 64.

8. *Renmin Ribao* [People's daily], March 9, 1978, pp. 1–5.

9. Chu-yüan Cheng, "The Modernization of Chinese Industry," in Richard Baum (ed.), *China's Four Modernizations: The New Technological Revolution* (Boulder, 1980), p. 26.

10. Chen Ting-chung, "Agricultural Modernization on the Chinese Mainland," in *Modernization Problems,* p. 16.

11. "Report on National Conference on Fundamental Farm Construction," *Renmin Ribao* [People's daily], Aug. 8, 1977.

12. Hu Qiaomu, "Observe Economic Laws, Speed Up the Four Modernizations," *Peking Review,* No. 47, Nov. 24, 1978, p. 18.

13. Chen Ting-chung, pp. 19–21. These figures are based on various mainland Chinese sources.

14. In Taiwan, it took US$11,000 to create a job opportunity during 1967–71. If Beijing could manage to create a job opportunity with half that amount, relocation of 100 million would cost $50 billion. *Ibid.,* p. 24.

15. *Ibid.,* p. 25.

16. These 27 fields include natural resources, agriculture, industry, defense, transportation, oceanography, environmental protection, medicine, finance, trade, culture, and education, in addition to a number of basic and technical sciences.

17. According to a study of the Royal Institute of International Affairs, London, by Lawrence Freedman entitled *The West and the Modernization of China* (London, 1979), p. 5, Chinese armed forces consisted of the following main units:

   STRATEGIC FORCES: medium-range ballistic missiles: 30–40 CSS–1, 600–700 miles; intermediate-range ballistic missiles: 30–40 CSS–2, 1750 miles;

[long-range ballistic missiles: some CSS–3, 3500 miles, first tested in 1976, and a small number of CSS-X-4, 6000–7000 miles, first tested in May 1980—author].

ARMY: 3,250,000 men, 10 armored divisions, 121 infantry divisions, and 150 independent regiments.

NAVY: 300,000 men, 30,000 Naval Air Force with 700 shore-based aircraft, 38,000 Marines, 23 major surface combat ships, and a rather large number of submarines and destroyers with missile-launching capability.

AIR FORCE: 400,000 men, 5,000 combat aircraft including some 4,000 MIG 17/19, and a small number of MIG 21 and F-9 fighters.

18. Cited in Freedman, 6.
19. Jonathan Pollack, "The Modernization of National Defense," in Baum (ed.), p. 247.
20. *Ibid.*, pp. 249–50.
21. Jeffrey Schultz, "The Four Modernizations Reconsidered," in Baum (ed.), p. 280.
22. Almon R. Roth, "Commentary on National Defense Modernization," in Baum (ed.), p. 262.
23. Pollack, pp. 255–56.
24. Hua Guofeng, "Report on the Work of the Government," *Peking Review*, No. 10, March 10, 1978, p. 23.
25. Pollack, p. 243.
26. Freedman, pp. 19–20.
27. *Ibid.*, p. 19.
28. The former figure given by Vice-Premier Li Xiannian, and the latter by Vice-Premier Deng Xiaoping.
29. Sun Yih, "Peiping's Plan for Defense Modernization," in *Modernization Problems*, p. 59.
30. *China: Economic Indicators* (Washington, D.C., 1978), p. 1.
31. Chu-yüan Cheng, in Baum (ed.), p. 37.
32. Hua Guofeng's report to the Fifth National People's Congress, First Session, Feb. 26, 1978, *Renmin Ribao* [People's daily], March 9, 1978.
33. Shannon R. Brown, "China's Program of Technology Acquisition," in Baum (ed.), p. 167.
34. *Ibid.*, pp. 165–66.
35. *American Banker*, April 19, 1979, quoted in Baum (ed.), p. 271.
36. Chu-yüan Cheng, in Baum (ed.), p. 38.
37. Cheng Chen-pang, "Tough Knots in Peiping's Four Modernizations," in *Modernization Problems*, pp. 80–81.
38. Zhou Peiyuan, president of Peking University and a vice-president of the Chinese Academy of Sciences.

39. Sun Yih, pp. 58–59.
40. Rudi Volti, "The Absorption and Assimilation of Acquired Technology," in Baum (ed.), p. 188.
41. Chu-yüan Cheng, "Industrial Modernization in China," *Current History*, Sept. 1980, p. 24.
42. *Peking Review*, No. 47, Nov. 24, 1978, pp. 17–21.
43. Chu-yüan Cheng, in Baum (ed.), p. 41; *Los Angeles Times*, May 10, 1979.
44. *Renmin Ribao* [People's daily], June 19, 1979; *Beijing Review*, No. 25, June 22, 1979, p. 11.
45. Chu-yüan Cheng, *Current History*, p. 25.
46. John Bryan Starr, "China's Economic Outreach," *Current History*, Sept. 1979, pp. 50–51.
47. Chu-yüan Cheng, *Current History*, p. 26.
48. *Ibid.*, p. 27.
49. *Ibid.*, p. 27.
50. *Renmin Ribao* [People's daily], Nov. 22, 1977.
51. Cheng Chu-yüan, "Chung-Kung Hsien-tai-hua ti tun-ts'o chi chan-wang" (The frustration of and prospect for Communist China's modernization), *Hai-wai hsüeh-jen* [Overseas scholars], Sept. 1980, 29.
52. *U.S. News & World Report*, March 23, 1981, pp. 56–58.
53. *Far East Times*, San Francisco, March 10, 1981.
54. *The Christian Science Monitor*, Feb. 20, 1981. Reportedly, the Japanese firm Mitsubishi Heavy Industries asked for an $84 million reparation.
55. *Hongqi* [Red flag], Beijing, No. 14, 1980, pp. 25–27.
56. *Renmin Ribao* [People's daily], July 1, 1980; Nov. 11, 1980; Feb. 24, 1981; *Guangming Daily*, March 28, 1981.
57. By 1990, oil production may reach 200 million tons; steel, 60 million tons; coal, 800 million tons; and foreign trade, $85 billion. Cheng Chu-yüan, "Chung-Kung hsien-tai-hua," pp. 31–32.
58. Liang Xiao, "The Yang Wu Movement and the Slavish Comprador Philosophy," *Historical Research*, No. 5, Oct. 20, 1975.
59. Genevieve C. Dean, "A Note on Recent Policy Changes," in Baum (ed.), p. 105.

FURTHER READING

Andors, Stephen, *China's Industrial Revolution: Politics, Planning, and Management, 1949 to the Present* (New York, 1977).
Baum, Richard (ed.), *China's Four Modernizations* (Boulder, 1980).

Bennett, Gordon, "Issues in China's Commercial and Financial Policy, 1978," *Contemporary China*, II:3:99–108 (Fall 1978).

Braybrooke, George, "Recent Development in Chinese Social Science, 1977–79," *The China Quarterly*, 79:593–601 (Sept. 1979).

Chang, Arnold, *Painting in the People's Republic of China: The Politics of Style* (Boulder, 1980).

Chen, Kuan-I, "Agricultural Modernization in China," *Current History*, 77:449:66–70, 85–86 (Sept. 1979).

Ch'en, Ting-chung, "Peiping's Ten-Year Economic Development Plan," *Issues & Studies*, XV:4:36–46 (April 1979).

Cheng, Chu-yüan, *China's Petroleum Industry: Output Growth and Export Potential* (New York, 1976).

———, "Industrial Modernization in China," *Current History*, 79:458:24–28, 43–44 (Sept. 1980).

———, "Chung-Kung hsien-tai-hua ti tun-ts'o chi chan-wang," (The frustration of and prospect for Communist China's modernization), *Hai-wai hsüeh-jen* [Overseas scholars], Sept. 1980, pp. 25–32.

Chinese Communist Modernization Problems (Taipei, Taiwan, 1979).

Chinn, Dennis L., "Basic Commodity Distribution in the People's Republic of China," *The China Quarterly*, 84:743–54 (Dec. 1980).

Chou, S. H., "Industrial Modernization in China," *Current History*, 77:449:49–52, 87–88 (Sept. 1979).

Dean, Genevieve C., *Science and Technology in the Development of Modern China: An Annotated Bibliography* (London, 1974).

———, and Fred Chernow, *The Choice of Technology in the Electronics Industry of the People's Republic of China: The Fabrication of Semiconductors* (Palo Alto, 1978).

Deng, Liqun, "Gongchan zhuyi shi qianqiu wandai de chonggao shiye" (Communism is a lofty calling for a myriad of generations), *Guangming Daily*, March 28, 1981.

Eckstein, Alexander, *China's Economic Revolution* (Cambridge, Eng., 1977).

———, *China's Economic Development: The Interplay of Scarcity and Ideology* (Ann Arbor, 1975).

Englesberg, Paul, "Education in Shanghai, 1976–1978," *Contemporary China*, III:2:69–78 (Summer 1979).

Field, Robert Michael, "A Slowdown in Chinese Industry," *The China Quarterly*, 80:734–39 (Dec. 1979).

Freedman, Lawrence, *The West and the Modernization of China*, Chatham House Papers (The Royal Institute of International Affairs, 1979).

Fureng, Dong, "Some Problems Concerning the Chinese Economy," *The China Quarterly*, 84:726–36 (Dec. 1980).

Gelber, Harry G., *Technology, Defense, and External Relations in China, 1975–1978* (Boulder, 1979).

Godwin, Paul H. B., "China and the Second World: The Search for Defense Technology," *Contemporary China*, II:3:3–9 (Fall 1978).

———, "China's Defense Dilemma: The Modernization Crisis of 1976 and 1977," *Contemporary China*, II:3:63–85 (Fall 1978).

———, *PLA-Military Forces of the PRC* (Boulder, 1981).

Goldman, Merle, "Teng Hsiao-p'ing and the Debate over Science and Technology," *Contemporary China*, II:4:46–69 (Winter 1978).

Hardy, Randall W., *China's Oil Future: A Case of Modest Expectations* (Boulder, 1978).

Harrison, Selig S., *China, Oil, and Asia: Conflict Ahead?* (New York, 1977).

Ho, Ping-ti, "China in the 1980's: Midway Toward Modernization," in Peter P. Cheng et al. (eds.), *Emerging Roles of Asian Nations in the Decade of the 1980's: A New Equilibrium* (Lincoln, 1979), pp. 8–46.

Howe, Christopher, *China's Economy: A Basic Guide* (New York, 1978).

Hu, Qiaomu, "Observe Economic Laws, Speed Up the Four Modernizations," Pt. I, *Peking Review*, 45:7–12 (Nov. 10, 1978); Pt. II, *Peking Review*, 46:15–23 (Nov. 17, 1978); Pt. III, *Peking Review*, 47:13–21 (Nov. 24, 1978).

Huang, Zhijian, "Jiujing yingdang ruhe renshi zhei yidai qingnian" (How shall we recognize this generation of youths?), *Renmin Ribao* [People's daily], Beijing, Feb. 24, 1981.

Huang, Philip C. C. (ed.), *The Development of Underdevelopment in China* (White Plains, N.Y., 1980).

"Integrating Moral Encouragement With Material Reward," *Peking Review*, 16:6–7 (April 21, 1978).

Klatt, W., "China's New Economic Policy: A Statistical Appraisal," *The China Quarterly*, 80:716–33 (Dec. 1979).

———, "China Statistics Up-dated," *The China Quarterly*, 84:737–43 (Dec. 1980).

Lardy, Nicholas R., "China's Economic Readjustment: Recovery or Paralysis?" in Robert B. Oxnam and Richard C. Bush (eds.), *China Briefing, 1980* (Boulder, 1980), pp. 39–51.

———, *Economic Growth and Distribution in China* (Cambridge, Eng., 1978).

——— (ed.), *Chinese Economic Planning: Translation from Chihua ching-chi* (White Plains, N.Y., 1979).

Li, Honglin, "Xinyang huiji shuoming liao shimo?" (What does the crisis of confidence mean?), *Renmin Ribao* [People's daily], Beijing, Nov. 11, 1980.

Li, K. T., "Mainland China's Economic Modernization: An Evaluation Based on Taiwan's Development Experience," *Issues & Studies*, XV:1:13–21 (July 1979).

Liu, Charles Y., "Problems in Estimating PRC Grain Production," *Contemporary China*, II:3:128–42 (Fall 1978).

MacDougall, Colina, "The Chinese Economy in 1976," *The China Quarterly*, 70:355–70 (June 1977).

Marwash, Onkar, and Jonathan D. Pollack (eds.), *Military Power and Policy in Asian States: China, India, Japan* (Boulder, 1979).

Myers, Ramon H., *The Chinese Economy: Past and Present* (Belmont, Calif., 1980).

National Foreign Assessment Center, *China: Economic Indicators* (Washington, D.C., Dec. 1978).

————, *China's Economy* (Washington, D.C., Nov. 1977).

————, *China: Gross Value of Industrial Output, 1965–77* (Washington, D.C., June 1978).

————, *China: In Pursuit of Economic Modernization* (Washington, D.C., Dec. 1978).

————, *China: Post-Mao Search for Civilian Industrial Technology* (Washington, D.C., 1979).

————, *China: The Continuing Search for a Modernization Strategy* (Washington, D.C., April 1980).

————, *China: A Statistical Compendium* (Washington, D.C., July 1979).

————, *China: The Steel Industry in the 1970s, anl 1980s* (Washington, D.C., 1979).

Nelsen, Harvey, *The Chinese Military System* (Boulder, 1981).

Pannell, Clifton W., and Christopher L. Salter (eds.), *China Geographer*, No. 11, *Agriculture* (Boulder, 1981).

Pollack, Jonathan, "The Modernization of National Defense," in Richard Baum (ed.), *China's Four Modernizations* (Boulder, 1980), pp. 241–61.

Prybyla, Jan. S., *The Chinese Economy: Problems and Policies* (Columbia, S.C., 1978).

————, "Feeding One Billion People: Agricultural Modernization in China," *Current History*, 79:458:19–23, 40–42 (Sept. 1980).

Reardon-Anderson, James, "Science and Technology in Post-Mao China," *Contemporary China*, II:4:37–45 (Winter 1978).

Sigurdson, Jon, *Rural Industrialization in China* (Cambridge, Mass., 1977).

Smil, Vaclav, *China's Energy Achievements, Problems, Prospects* (New York, 1976).

——, "The Energy Cost of China's Modernization," *Contemporary China,* II:3:109–114 (Fall 1978).

Stavis, Benedict, *Making Green Revolution—The Politics of Agricultural Development in China* (Ithaca, 1974).

Stover, Leon E., *The Cultural Ecology of Chinese Civilization: Peasant Elites in the Last of the Agrarian States* (Stanford, 1979).

Suttmeier, Richard P., *Research and Revolution: Science Policy and Societal Change in China* (Lexington, Mass., 1974).

—— et al., *Science and Technology in the People's Republic of China* (Paris, 1977).

——, *Science, Technology and China's Drive for Modernization* (Stanford, 1981).

Swetz, Frank, *Mathematics Education in China: Its Growth and Development* (Cambridge, Mass., 1974).

Ullerich, Curtis, *Rural Employment and Manpower Problems in China* (White Plains, N.Y., 1979).

Unger, Jonathan, "China's Troubled Down-to-the-Countryside Campaign," *Contemporary China,* III:2:79–92 (Summer 1979).

Volti, Rudi, *Science and Technology in China* (Boulder, 1981).

Wang, K. P., *Mineral Resources and Basic Industries in the People's Republic of China* (Boulder, 1977).

Wiens, Thomas B., "China's Agricultural Targets: Can They Be Met?" *Contemporary China,* II:3:115–127 (Fall 1978).

5

The End of the Maoist Age

THE TRIAL OF THE GANG OF FOUR
AND THE LIN BIAO GROUP

An unprecedented legal and political event took place in China from November 1980 to January 1981: the trial of the Gang of Four and the associates of Lin Biao. In the past, political dissidents or opponents defeated in power struggles were summarily purged, imprisoned, liquidated, or made "non-persons." But the new leadership, to show that China was entering an era of emphasis on the rule of law in which sentences would be rendered only after guilt was proven by trial, established a special court to try the Jiang Qing and Lin Biao groups for crimes allegedly committed against the state and the people. It was extremely difficult to prepare for the trial because of its political ramification; yet the leadersip decided to proceed in order to symbolize the beginning of a new order.

The four-year interval between the arrest of the Gang and the opening of the trial indicated the sensitivity and complexity of the issues at stake and the intensity of intraparty debate over the wisdom of and procedure for such an undertaking.

The crux of the matter was Mao's intimate involvement in the rise of the Gang and its activities. Should he be implicated in the trial it would be necessary to have an official party assessment of his role during and after the Cultural Revolution in order to get at the truth of the matter. Yet no quick consensus could be reached due to vast differences in the opinions held by various leaders; to await such an assessment would further delay the trial. In addition, the position of Chairman Hua Guofeng was extremely sensitive due to his role as minister of public security (and later premier) while the Gang held sway over national policies. It was entirely possible, even inevitable, that he would be named as a witness at the trial. Thus, the question of separating Mao and Hua from the trial became a key issue in the high councils of state, one which could not be resolved without prolonged debate, intense negotiating, and many compromises.

Pretrial Politics

After their arrest in October 1976, the Four were repeatedly interrogated by government investigators in hopes of collecting evidence, confessions, and any relevant information as a basis for formal charges. But all four were crafty politicians and skillfully dodged questions, passing all responsibility for their actions to Mao. In May 1980 the party held a secret pretrial hearing of the Four. Jiang Qing vigorously protested her innocence by insisting that her every act was carried out under express orders from Mao with the approval of the party Central Committee. Mao's only mistake, she said, was his choice of Hua as premier, for it whetted Hua's appetite for higher positions; and in the end he betrayed Mao's teaching and surrendered to capitalist countries in the manner of Li Hongzhang a century earlier. She insisted that Hua had been not only fully aware and supportive of her activities but was actually deeply involved (as minister of public security) in the suppression of the April 5, 1976, Tian An Men Square Incident; hence he must be called as a witness at the trial.[1]

Wang Hongwen and Zhang Chunqiao likewise attributed

all responsibility for their actions to Mao, indicating further that Hua, as an insider, knew the full story. Yao Wenyuan's defense differed only slightly, holding the party center responsible and criticizing the current leadership for deviation from Mao's line in pursuing the Four Modernizations with the co-operation of foreign capitalists. In short, all four involved Mao and Hua in their defense.

Within the party leadership two lines of thought quickly emerged. General Secretary Hu Yaobang and party Vice-Chairman Chen Yun argued that only by first assessing Mao's contributions and mistakes could the crimes of the Gang be properly fixed. If Mao had not ignored "party democracy" and sponsored the Gang's rise to power, how could the Four have done such atrocious harm to the country? On the other hand, Hua and his supporters argued that any assessment of Mao's responsibility before the trial would lighten the responsibility of the Gang for its crimes; the inevitable inference would be that Mao and the party would bear the ultimate burden. They asked for an assessment of the Gang's crimes before an assessment of Mao.

To avoid further delay, the leadership finally decided that the trial should go ahead as announced without first making an assessment of Mao's role. Several guiding principles were adopted, the most basic of which was, according to Vice-Chairman Deng, to distinguish "political mistakes or misjudgments" from the actual crimes of murder, illegal detention, and torture. Mao's role in the Cultural Revolution was seen as a "mistake," not a "crime"; hence he could not be indicted. The other principles adopted were:

1. The trial was to be held in secret in order to prevent the disclosure of "state secrets" that might be revealed during the proceedings.
2. Great effort would be made to separate Mao from the Gang; the less he was mentioned the better. The crimes of the Four would be determined first so as to retain flexibility in the assessment of Mao.
3. Although the Four behaved as a group and committed similar crimes, the degree of responsibility varied and hence

their penalties must be graded. Jiang Qing was the chief culprit, followed by Zhang Chunqiao and Yao Wenyuan, while Wang Hongwen, a young upstart who joined the Gang seeking rapid promotions (and who showed repentance during interrogation) was assessed last in the order of crimes and punishments.[2]

Even without a pretrial assessment of Mao, Hua remained in a most uncomfortable position. Although Hua, after Mao's death and in conjunction with party and military leaders, had engineered a "palace revolution" to topple the Gang, he was nonetheless a beneficiary of the Cultural Revolution and had been favored by Mao in his naming as premier and then as "anointed successor." Therefore he was not anxious to hold the trial and dreaded being called as a witness, but he could not openly oppose the trial. His tactics were to delay it as long as possible while secretly working out an "understanding" with the other power holders. Reportedly, he demanded that these four conditions be met:

1. The trial should not implicate Wang Dongxing and his associates in the crimes of the Cultural Revolution. (In other words, Hua would not appear as witness.)
2. The trial should not involve the Tian An Men Square Incident.
3. The trial should not involve the "Criticize Deng, Antirightist Deviationist Campaign."
4. No sentence of immediate execution should be given to Jiang Qing.[3]

These conditions seemed sufficient to protect Hua from the worst of the predictable criticisms that the trial might stir up.

With these guidelines and "understandings" established, the leaders were ready to open the trial. A Special Court of thirty-five judges was created in which there were two sections: a civil tribunal for the Gang of Four and a military tribunal for the six associates of Lin Biao. Since the Lin group was accused of plotting against Mao, while the Gang was charged with usurping state power and party leadership under the aegis of

Mao, the logic of combining the two groups in one trial seemed questionable. But the government rationalized that the two groups had conspired together during the Cultural Revolution in an attempt to overthrow the proletarian dictatorship, and in doing so they severely hurt the country, the people, and the present leaders. Ironically, both groups happened to have been favored by Mao at one time or another, and both had failed in attempts to seize supreme power.

Like the Nuremberg and Tokyo Trials after World War II, the trial in question was in fact a "victor's trial" held in response to a popularly felt need for justice.[4] What remained to be seen was whether the court was in fact a court of law or just a legal arm of the Politburo.

The Trial

On November 20, 1980, the long-awaited trial was formally opened by Jiang Hua, chief justice of the Supreme Court. The other thirty-four judges included military men, politicians, and well-known intellectuals;[5] seven of them had no legal training but were "special assessors" brought in to express the people's condemnation of the Cultural Revolution and the Gang. No foreign correspondents were admitted, and only 880 selected Chinese representatives chosen from provincial and government organizations, the party, and the army were admitted in a system of rotation.

The spotlight, of course, was on the star defendant, Jiang Qing, sixty-seven, who strode into the courtroom haughtily. Wearing a shiny black wig, she was immaculately clothed in black—a color said to symbolize the injustice that had been inflicted upon her, and perhaps also her grief over the demise of the leftist ideology she had once personified. Of the remaining Gang members, Zhang Chunqiao, sixty-three, looked weary, defiant, and older than his years; Yao Wenyuan, forty-nine, had grown fatter; while Wang Hongwen, forty-five, appeared hesitant, perhaps a result of his cooperation with the prosecution in what might be called "plea bargaining." Other co-defendants included Chen Boda, seventy-six, Mao's former political secretary who defected to Lin Biao and was purged in 1970, and five generals associated with Lin.[6] Sitting behind the iron bars of the prisoner's dock with downcast faces and uneasy demeanors suggesting long years in prison, they looked unkempt, haggard, and old. Only Jiang Qing appeared proud and strong, staring at the judges and prosecutors with utter contempt.

First, Special Prosecutor Huang Huoqing, head of the State Procuratorate, named six deceased persons who, if alive, would have been prosecuted as co-defendants: Lin Biao, his wife and son, a follower killed in the 1971 air crash, Kang Sheng (Mao's former security head), and his successor, Xie Fuzhi. Pointedly unnamed was Mao, who nevertheless was viewed by many as an "unindicted defendant" of a "Gang of Five."

Then Huang read a 20,000-word indictment charging the defendants with usurpation of state power and party leadership. Their chief crimes fell into four major categories:

1. Framing and persecuting party and state leaders and plotting to overthrow the proletarian dictatorship.
2. Persecuting, killing, and torturing a large number of cadres and masses in excess of 34,375 people.
3. Plotting an armed uprising in Shanghai after Mao's death, with Wang Hongwen in charge of distributing 300 cannon, 74,000 rifles, and 10 million rounds of bullets to the militia in August 1976.
4. Plotting to assassinate Mao and to stage an armed counter-revolutionary coup.

The first two caegories applied to all ten defendants; the third to the Gang, and the fourth to the Lin Biao group. Forty-eight specific charges of crimes as legally defined, which did not include ideological or political mistakes. were made.[7]

During the trial, Jiang Qing rejected the services of three government-appointed lawyers on the grounds that they disagreed with her line of defense and could not properly represent her. She chose to speak for herself, and this former actress came close to the best performance of her life. She assumed a studied posture of innocence and composure mingled with a pride and arrogance that suggested a "regal" disdain for the entire proceedings. She tried to project the image of a revolutionary martyr—a Chinese Joan of Arc—whose only crime was defeat in a political struggle. All her actions, she insisted, were carried out on the express orders of Mao with the approval of the Central Committee. How else could she have done as she did? Many Chinese who called her a "witch" and "the most hated in the world" secretly agreed with her, and even conceded in private that she had an "indomitable spirit." Mao was the real culprit, they reasoned, for without him she could never have become what she was.

Jiang was accused of being the chief instigator of a plot to send Wang Hongwen to see Mao in October 1974 to falsely accuse Premier Zhou Enlai of suspicious meetings with other leaders and to block his appointment of Deng as first vice-premier. She responded to the charge contemptuously: "No, I don't know (anything about that). How would I know that?" The prosecutor then called Wang to testify. He admitted that the Four did meet at Jiang Qing's residence in Beijing (the Angler's Guest House) in October 1974 to plot the defamation of Zhou and Deng, adding, "It was Jiang Qing who called (us) together and the purpose was to prevent Deng from becoming first vice-premier." Wang further implicated Yao Wenyuan by stating that Yao pressed him to tell Mao that the situation in Beijing then was critical, much like that at the August 1970 Lushan Conference when Lin Biao attempted a coup. Yao did not deny his part, but emphasized that it was Jiang Qing who organized the plan to frame Zhou and Deng. The other witnesses, Mao's niece Wang Hairong (a vice-minister of foreign affairs) and Nancy Tang (Mao's favorite English translator), testified that Jiang Qing had asked them to defame Zhou and Deng before Mao, but they had refused.

Jiang Qing's response to all this was a look of utter unconcern. At one point, she declared that the charges against her involved a "contradiction among the people," i.e. an outcome of political differences and not of criminal or counterrevolutionary activities. But the chief justice accepted the prosecution's argument that the evidence was "sufficient" and

Jiang Qing at the Trial of the Gang of Four.

"conclusive" that the Jiang Qing Group (now replacing the term the "Gang of Four") framed Zhou and Deng to create favorable conditions for themselves to usurp party leadership and state power.

Wang Hongwen in the dock during the Trial.

The Group was also accused of illegally prosecuting three-quarters of a million people and killing 34,375 of them during the decade of 1966–76. To prove the crimes, the prosecution projected on a large screen grisly pictures of the badly bruised corpse of a former minister of coal mining and played chilling tape recordings of screaming, wailing, and moaning from intellectuals who refused to cooperate with Jiang Qing and were abused in her private torture chamber.[8]

Chen Boda, assumed dead since his purge in 1970, appeared feeble and old. He admitted having plotted with Jiang Qing and Kang Sheng in July 1967 the purge of Liu Shaoqi and his death in prison. Chen further confessed to ordering the purges of Deng Xiaoping (then party general secretary), Tao Zhu (Canton party leader), and Lu Dingyi (party Propaganda Department head). In late 1967 Chen even had pressed false charges against Zhu De, the co-founder of the Red Army and chairman of the National People's Congress. In all, Chen was charged with wrongful persecution of 84,000 people and the deaths of 2,950 during the Cultural Revolution.

Under repreated questioning, Jiang Qing broke down and admitted that she wrote letters to a group in charge of the persecution of Liu Shaoqi, instructing that Liu be hounded to death."[9] This irrefutably incriminating testimony enabled the prosecution to score a major breakthrough in the trial.

As time wore on Jiang Qing was increasingly affected by the pressures of the trial and began to lose her studied composure. When Wang Hongwen told the court that Mao had warned him "Don't hang around with Jiang Qing," she visibly squirmed. When party writer Liao Mosha, former director of the Beijing Municipal United Front Department purged in 1968, sobbingly testified that he had been imprisoned for eight years and subjected to brutal and inhuman tortures on false charges of being a "fierce secret agent," Jiang Qing angrily shouted at him: "Stop acting! You are a renegade!" When the judges ordered her to stop shouting, she jeered, "I have already spoken. What are you going to do about it?" For her contempt of court, an ejection order was issued. The female bailiffs pushed and pulled her down the aisle, while the spectators broke into thunderous applause.[10]

December 23 saw another stormy session of shouting matches. The witness, Ah Jia, former deputy director of the Beijing Opera Theater, accused Jiang Qing of stealing his opera "The Red Lantern," turning it into one of her own revolutionary model productions, and then persecuting him as a counterrevolutionary so that he could not reveal her plagiarism. He turned to Jiang Qing in court and said: "You were once very high but you are low and despicable. . . . Your heart is vicious and your means are ruthless. You have a sordid soul." Jiang Qing totally lost control, shouting at Ah Jia and calling the judges and the prosecutors "facists" and "legal quibblers" and everyone else members of the Kuomintang.

In a final move to prove Jiang Qing's guilt, the prosecution produced a list of Central Committee members prepared by her for purge during the Cultural Revolution: Liu Shaoqi, Deng Xiaoping, Marshal He Long, Marshal Peng Dehuai, and Mayor Peng Zhen of Beijing. History showed that all of them had been forced out of office, the prosecution asserted, and all on false charges brought by Jiang Qing.

As regards the six defendants of the Lin Biao Group, all pleaded guilty to the charge that they plotted the murder of Mao while he was touring the country in September 1971, on orders from Lin. The oldest of them, Chen Boda, expressed the sentiments of all six when he said that he had nothing to say in his own defense, but that he asked for mercy from the party.

After twenty-seven days of trial and many recesses extending nearly two months, the court concluded its work on December 29, 1980, without announcing a verdict. Eight of the ten defendants admitted their guilt as charged, but Zhang Chunqiao consistently refused to coperate and Jiang Qing remained unrepentant to the end. At the final session she broke into a blaze of rhetoric, defending the Cultural Revolution, her role as Mao's wife for thirty-eight years, and her obedience to the orders of Mao and of the Central Committee. It was the present leadership, she charged, that deviated from the socialist line and practiced revisionism. "When you vilify me, you are vilifying Chairman Mao and the Cultural Revolution in which millions of people participated," she proclaimed, hoping to rally the support of opponents of the current leadership. She condemned the judges, the prosecution, and political leaders as reactionaries, counterrevolutionaries, and fascists.[11]

Prosecutor Jiang Wen asked that Jiang Qing be given a severe penalty (though not necessarily death) in view of her "particularly serious, particularly wicked" counterrevolutionary activities. He came close to condemning Mao when he said, "The people of all nationalities throughout the country understand that Chairman Mao was responsible, so far as his leadership was concerned, for their plight during the Cultural Revolution, and that he was also responsible for failing to see through the Lin Biao and Jiang Qing counterrevolutionary cliques." Nonetheless, the prosecutor was quick to add, Mao made great contributions toward overthrowing imperialism, feudalism, and bureaucratic-capitalism, and was responsible for the founding of the People's Republic and for pioneering the socialist cause in China. Echoing the views of Deng, the prosecutor said that Mao's achievements were primary and his mistakes secondary.[12]

Still feisty, unrepentant, and haughty, Jiang Qing shouted in the court: "Fine. Go ahead! You can't kill Mao—he is already dead—but you can kill me. Still I regret nothing. I was right!" Declaring it would be more glorious to have her head chopped off than to yield to her accusers, she told the court: "I dare you to sentence me to death in front of one million people in Tian An Men Square."

Ultimately, just as the trial was political, so the verdict had to reflect the views of the present leadership; and a consensus was not reached for three weeks. From the legal standpoint, Article 103 of the new criminal code prescribes death for those who commit "serious crimes" against the state, but from the political standpoint, was execution the best course to take? Pragmatic leaders such as Deng and Hu and most of the public seem to favor immediate execution to clear the air, to repudiate the Cultural Revolution and the Mao cult, to satisfy all those who had been victimized by the Gang, and to use the occasion to mark a new dedication to the drive for modernization. Hua Guofeng (who had announced a year earlier that there would be no execution) opposed the death sentence, and large numbers of Maoists considered executing the widow of the founder of the People's Republic too great an affront to Mao.

A compromise solution was offered by party Vice-Chairman Chen Yun, who argued that execution would lift Jiang Qing's position to that of a Maoist revolutionary martyr and perhaps goad the 18 million party members who had joined during and after the Cultural Revolution into a second cultural revolution, creating the danger of a party split and large-scale disturbances. Chen reminded the party that at sixty-seven Jiang Qing would not have many more years to live. A suspended death sentence followed by a long period of confinement in a remote security prison would gradually obliterate her from people's memories. The party leaders, who had long been wrestling with this complex dilemma, accepted this approach.[13]

On January 25, 1981, the Special Court announced the death sentence for Jiang Qing and Zhang Chunqiao, but with a two-year suspended execution. Jiang Qing, apparently surprised at the verdict or misunderstanding the meaning of a suspended sentence, immediately denounced the judges, shouting, "To rebel is justified; revolution is no crime! Down with revisionists headed by Deng Xiaoping!" Armed female bailiffs quickly snapped handcuffs on her and hustled her out of the court.

In spite of Wang Hongwen's cooperation and the original low assessment of his responsibility and punishment, he was given life imprisonment. Yao Wenyuan received twenty years and Chen Boda, eighteen years imprisonment. The other five generals were sentenced to sixteen to eighteen years in jail. With the exception of Yao, forty-nine, most are not likely to survive the long sentences.

Looking at the excruciatingly long time that it took the leadership to reach their verdict, one can only be reminded of the still powerful influence of the patriarch Mao. In life he sponsored the rise of his wife, and in death he shielded her from immediate execution. Jiang Qing seemed to know the present leadership dared not repudiate Mao and the Ninth and Tenth Party Congresses without severely discrediting the party itself. Indeed, her main line of defense was never directly refuted by the prosecution. But her role in the persecution and deaths of 34,375 people and her maintenance of a private torture chamber were unforgivable crimes, for which even a death sentence seemed too charitable. Yet the verdict, like the trial itself, was politically motivated and would be politically decided. The specter of Mao inhibited the present leadership from killing her.

Some Questions about the Trial

Legal practice, procedure, and terminology in China are very different from those of the West. A defendant in the West is presumed innocent until proven guilty. In China, law has always operated on the assumption that unless a man were guilty of something he would not be arrested in the first place. Western legal terminology clearly differentiates between a "suspect" and a "criminal"; in China an apprehended man is often referred to as a criminal even before judicial determination of his involvement in a crime. Thus, in the present trial the ten defendants were called "major criminals" (*zhufan*) in the indictment, implicitly connoting a prejudgment.

Furthermore, the role of the Special Court was never clearly defined. Was it to determine the guilt or innocence of the defendants, or to fix the degree of guilt of each, or to carry out the orders of the party? From the start everybody knew that the trial was legal in form but political in reality; hence the arguments of the prosecution and the final verdict of the court had to reflect the views of the political leadership. Moreover, while a trial without a jury is quite common in China, the fact that the thirty-five judges outnumbered the defendants by three to one was most unusual even by Chinese standards.

In the political context, the government leaders who wanted the trial and the court president and the chief prosecutor had all been victims of the Cultural Revolution. Could the trial of their former oppressors be impartially carried out without personal vengeance? In the West these judges and prosecutors would most likely have disqualified themselves on the grounds of a "conflict of interests."

In terms of judicial procedures, seven of the thirty-five judges had not legal training at all, raising the question of their qualification. Several of them were called "special assessors" and acted as "silent jurors" rather than judges. The Chinese legal profession, suppressed since 1957, had only recently been revived, and it is understandable that there was a shortage of properly trained legal personnel. But to fill judgeships with persons who have no legal training is a questionable judicial act.

Another procedural question involves the criminal code in which the charges were based, which came into effect on January 1, 1980. Was it legal to apply it retroactively to crimes committed ten to fifteen years earlier?

Finally, the major political obstacle in the trial was the role of Mao. Though unnamed in the indictment, from the final statement of the prosecution it was clear that Mao was largely responsible (as the national leader) for failing to recognize the evil work of the two accused groups and of their effect on the people. It was a tactful way to suggest that Mao was too great to be indicted openly, yet too involved to be dismissed completely. As a young Chinese put it, "It really should be the Gang of Five, but we cannot afford to defile the father-figure yet."[14] This statement contains much truth and probably expresses the feeling of a great many people.

In a sense, the trial may be viewed as an indirect trial of Mao, with Jiang Qing serving as his surrogate. To probe still deeper, one may say that the trial was an indictment of the entire system which allowed Mao to overpower the Central Committee and allowed his wife's group to drive the country to the brink of anarchy and economic disaster. The net effect of the trial was a further erosion of the image of Mao and the effectiveness of the system he created.

The implied censure of Mao's role in his later years points up China's current crisis of a lack of "faith, trust, and confidence" in both leaders and party. Chinese youths who lived through the Cultural Revolution became alarmingly cynical and disillusioned, as one ex-Red Guard recalled: "They told us [the Cultural Revolution] was a class struggle. . . . It was not until this year that I realized the Cultural Revolution was really a power struggle, not a class struggle."[15] One writer confided to a foreign correspondent: "To have done things really fairly, the whole Central Committee would have to go on trial, since it approved of the Cultural Revolution. The worst criminal [in this] was Mao."[16]

In spite of all its shortcomings, the trial was a positive step forward—to quote government leaders, a "milestone" in the emerging order of a rule of law. It was important for people to see that one could differ with the government without facing a firing squad; at the same time, it satisfied a widely felt need to censure the leadership and excesses of the Cultural Revolution.

A not unexpected repercussion of the trial was its adverse effect on the future of Chairman Hua. As minister of public security during the heyday of the Gang, he signed warrants authorizing arrests, prison sentences, and even deaths for enemies of the Gang, for which some said he should be held responsible. During the trial, dialogues occasionally went beyond the prescribed script and implicated him in the "Criticize Deng, Antirightist Deviationist" Campaign and in the suppression of the Tian An Men Square Incident as well. The Dengists were quick to exploit the situation by accusing him of practicing "personality cultism" after the smashing of the Gang and of mismanaging modernization programs by stressing revolutionary zeal over solid economic planning. The Dengists saw Hua's leadership as a continuation of "wrong" Maoist policy which might provide a future rallying point for disaffected ultraleftists to oppose the coure of the persent leadership. Great pressure was exerted on him to resign.

Reportedly, Hua offered to resign as party chairman at the November 1980 meeting of the Politburo, to be effective at the next plenum of the party Central Committee in June 1981. Though still chairman until then, Hua had been reduced to a figurehead. The real power of the party fell into the hands of General Secretary Hu Yaobang, and Deng Xiaoping became the de facto chairman of the Military Commission. While no one denies Hua's key role in smashing the Gang, Chinese newspapers increasingly report that credit for such an exploit "should not go to individuals but to the rules of historical development and to the will of the people."[17] With the phasing out of Hua, the Maoist age came closer to an end.

The main lesson of the trial is that Chinese leadership must take heed of the defects in their system which allowed one of the gravest misfortunes in Chinese history to occur. Unless corrective measures are devised to prevent its recurrence, instability will continue to plague Chinese politics and block genuine progress. China cannot afford to lose any more time in its drive to become a modernized state.

ASSESSMENTS OF MAO

Few issues in Chinese politics have caused such deep dissension as the assessment of Mao. The pragmatic leaders, the victims of the Cultural Revolution and the Gang of Four, and a considerable number of youths favored a candid and critical assessment of Mao's achievements and failings. They regarded his legacy as unfit for the new mission of modernization and cited his failure to lift China from poverty as proof of the inadequacy of his approach. On the other hand, a large number of party and military leaders and cadres who owed their status to Mao's revolution, particularly the "old-timers" and those who rose during the Cultural Revolution, considered such an assessment tantamount to a defamation of the man who led the revolution to success, founded the People's Republic, and pioneered the socialist cause in China. Sympathetic to this latter view were many others who grew up under the influence of ceaseless indoctrination that Mao saved China from imperialism, feudalism, and capitalism, and gave the people a new life. These people could not easily renounce their habitual reverence of the Leader.

In the vortex of such conflicting views, consensus was difficult to reach; the closest thing to it was Vice-Chairman Deng's statement that Mao achievements were primarily and his mistakes secondary. The party adopted the principle of separating Mao's thought from Mao's leadership qualities. Mao's thought is said to represent the sum total of the Chinese revolutionary experience: all the contributions made by all the participants in that revolution. Hence it does not reflect Mao's thinking alone but is the legacy of all Chinese, and they must continue to treasure it. On the other hand, Mao as a leader made many contributions as well as some very serious mistakes. To assess his achievements and errors impartially is to seek truth from facts and to learn from past experiences. Despite its compromising nature, the party's critical position was unacceptable to some. The elder statesman and military leader Ye Jianying, for example, showed his displeasure by leaving Beijing for Guangzhou in late 1980 on "sick leave." He still retained considerable influence among the military and may have used it to affect the assessment of Mao.

General Huang's View

The first open assessment of Mao came in April 1981 from General Huang Kecheng, who as chief of general staff of the Liberation Army had been purged in 1959, along with Defense Minister Peng Dehuai, and had not been rehabilitated until 1977. Now an executive secretary of the party's Central Commission for Inspecting Discipline, his assessment perhaps represented the army view. It is a generous and sympathetic review of Mao's accomplishments vis-à-vis his mistakes and a eulogy to the Thought of Mao. The prominence with which Huang's article was published suggests that a party-approved compromise had been reached between military and political leaders, and that the pragmatists had made certain concessions in order to reach a consensus. Huang's long article may well have been a preview of the formal party assessment, published in advance to test public reactions.

General Huang enumerated Mao's achievements, beginning with the Autumn Uprising in 1927, to the founding of the Red Army and the Chinese Soviet government, the Long March, ending with the ultimate seizure of power in 1949. He pointed to these achievements as evidence of Mao's major role in founding the party and the People's Republic and in steering the revolution through many crises. As Deng had stated, "Without Mao the Chinese people would have had to grope in the dark for a much longer time." However, the assessment did not deny the contributions of others, or suggest that Mao was China's "savior."

In General Huang's assessment, after Liberation, Mao correctly launched the land revolution, entered the Korean War to fight American aggression, implemented the three major transformations (agriculture, handicrafts, and capitalist industry and commerce), and initiated the socialist revolution and construction of the nation.

Yet, in his later years Mao committed many mistakes, and Huang viewed two as particularly serious. The first was that having established a socialist government and completed the three major transformations, Mao failed to decisively shift the major task of government and party to socialist construction. Simultaneously, he was rash and reckless in seeking unrealistic results in socialist revolution and construction. Secondly, he blurred the two distinct types of contradictions, treating those within the party as if they were enemies outside it: thus class struggle was carried to the extreme, and opportunities were created for bad elements to exploit divisions and initiate the disastrous Cultural Revolution.

In Huang's view, however, these mistakes were not Mao's alone, but should be shared. During the Great Leap of 1958, many comrades were guilty of setting unrealistic targets and exaggerating facts and figures, and they were responsible for exacerbating the already serious problems. The Central Committee itself must also be held responsible for the many erroneous resolutions it passed. If the old comrades shared Mao's glory in good times, they must also share the burden of his mistakes. While Mao, as chairman, should be assessed the ultimate responsibility, it would be grossly unfair to heap all the blame on one man alone. Only by learning from past mistakes could the living carry on the unfinished task of Mao to serve the country and the people.

Huang diagnosed several reasons for Mao's failures. First, to build socialism without experience in a poor, backward, and extremely populous country was a most difficult task. Even today, the Chinese are still groping for solutions to many problems, and new mistakes are inevitable. In addition, in Mao's later years he became less prudent, less democratic, and less aware of the masses and the reality of the country. Having worked all his life for revolution, he was tired and overwrought, and therefore prone to mistakes and a distorted sense of proportion. Mao was racing against time, hoping to accomplish in a few decades what would normally take several hundred years to achieve. While the result was confusion and failure, his intentions were good; hence he must be viewed with sympathy and understanding. To defame him would defame the party and the socialist motherland.

In conclusion, Huang delved into a long discourse on Maoism as a spiritual weapon not to be discarded lightly. Neither Confucianism, nor the Three People's Principles, but only the Thought of Mao could serve socialist China; for it is the creative transmutation of Marxism-Leninism to the specific conditions of China and as such has distinctive Chinese characteristics. Moreover, the Thought of Mao has been repeatedly affirmed in party constitutions; to negate it would violate the constitution. To be sure, not every word of Mao's was correct and not every concept up-to-date, but the essence of the Thought should serve as a spiritual guide, to be continuously enriched and developed by later generations.[18]

General Huang's assessment is significant for its omissions as well as its content. Mao's successful dealings with the Soviets were omitted, including the very substantial aid program that resulted in one of the largest technological transfers in modern history and was the foundation of early Chinese industrialization. Nor was there any acknowledgment of his skillful recovery of the Soviet Manchurian "loot" and claims to joint ventures in Xinjiang. These substantial diplomatic gains should hardly be ignored, regardless of current Sino-Soviet enmity.

In the assessment, nineteen paragraphs are devoted to a recital of Mao's successes before 1949, compared with a three-line paragraph on his later achievements. The long list of Mao's achievements from 1927 to 1949 is never doubted; he is universally recognized as the greatest revolutionary of the mid-twentieth century. What is in question is his statemanship and the quality of his leadership after 1949. Chinese leaders have frankly admitted that only the first seven years of the People's republic were "good" years and that the next twenty were chaotic.[19] Even in those early years, the decision to enter the Korean War was at best questionable, for it cost China dearly at a time domestic reconstruction needed capital desperately.

The Antirightist Movement of 1957, which sacrificed hundreds of thousands of intellectuals and devastated China's cultural and artistic development, marked the beginning of Mao's erratic leadership. The Great Leap was precipitous. The introduction of communes was premature, forcing farmers into unfamiliar ways of production and driving millions to starvation. The fight with Defense Minister Peng in 1959, a storm in a teapot, held disastrous implications of the Leader's omnipotence, while the power struggle with Liu Shaoqi, dignified under the name of Cultural Revolution, opened the way for a decade of disorder and the disastrous rise of the Gang of Four. Suffice it to say that an impartial assessment should have taken into account these occurrences, good intentions notwithstanding, and critically discussed the glorification of the Thought of Mao which had obstructed the prevention of such mistakes. Moreover, one must question Huang's emphasis on the "spiritual weapon" in a system dedicated to dialectical materialism.

Mao's position in history, as viewed by present party leadership, was revealed in a *Renmin Ribao* [People's daily] article (March 19, 1981) entitled "Patriotism as a Great Spiritual Power in Building Socialism" which listed "outstanding personalities" in Chinese history. The list included the philosophers Lao-tzu, Confucius, and Mencius; Tang poets Li Po and Tu Fu; and the emperors Liu Bang, Tang Taizong, and Genghis Khan. Among modern personalities, Emperor Kangxi, Hong Xiuquan, Kang Youwei, and Sun Yat-sen were mentioned with more recent leaders such as Li Dazhao, Qu Qiubai, Mao Zedong, Zhou Enlai, Zhu De, and Peng Dehuai. Thus, in what might be called the Chinese Communist "Hall of Fame," Mao's historical model, the First Emperor of Qin, was absent, and

Mao himself ranked third among Communist leaders, preceded by the dubious character Qu and followed by Marshal Peng whom Mao had disgraced.

The Party Assessment

The long-awaited party assessment of Mao finally came at the Sixth Plenary Session of the Eleventh Central Committee held between June 27 and 29, 1981. In a leadership reshuffle, the plenum accepted Hua Guofeng's resignation, naming Hu Yaobang chairman of the Central Committee, and Deng Xiaoping chairman of the Military Commission, thereby breaking the tradition of one man holding both posts. Another personnel change was the appointment of Premier Zhao Ziyang as a vice-chairman of the party, forming a "collective triumvirate" with Hu and Deng. Hua Guofeng became the most junior of the six vice-chairmen, a powerless but nevertheless respectable position.[20]

The plenum adopted a 35,000-word "Resolution on Certain Questions in the History of Our Party Since the Founding of the People's Republic," which detailed the party's accomplishments in the past sixty years, especially since 1949. However, a major point of the document was the Cultural Revolution and Mao's role in it. The party's stand was unequivocally critical: "The 'Great Cultural Revolution' from May 1966 to October 1976 caused the most devastating setback and heavy losses to the party, the state, and the people in the history of the People's Republic, and this 'Great Cultural Revolution' was initiated and led by Comrade Mao Zedong."

The movement, said the party, was neither in conformity with the thought of Mao nor with Marxism-Leninism or the realities of China. Indeed, the assertion that the "Great Cultural Revolution" was a struggle against revisionism and capitalism was, in retrospect, groundless. False accusations were prevalent: the "capitalist roaders" who were knocked down were in fact leaders from different levels of the party and the government who were the core force of socialist construction; the so-called "Liu-Deng Bourgeois Headquarters" never really existed. The persecution of "reactionary intellectual authorities" sacrificed countless talented and accomplished scholars. Moreover, the Cultural Revolution was conducted in the name of the masses but was actually divorced from both the party and the masses. Pointedly, the document stated: "Comrade Mao's leftist mistakes and personal leadership actually replaced the collective leadership of the party center and he became the object of fervent personal worship." The prominence of Mao's errors made a critical assessment absolutely necessary, for "to overlook mistakes or to whitewash them is not only impermissible but is in itself a mistake." The verdict was:

> Practice has shown that the "Great Cultural Revolution" did not in fact institute a revolution or social progress in any sense, nor could it possibly have done so. It was we and not the enemy who were thrown into disorder by it. Therefore, from beginning to end, it did not turn "great disorder under heaven" into "great order under heaven." . . . History has shown that the "Great Cultural Revolution," initiated by a leader laboring under a misconception and capitalized on by counter-revolutionary cliques, led to domestic turmoil and brought catastrophe to the party, the state, and the whole people. . . . Comrade Mao . . . far from making a correct analysis of many problems . . . confused right and wrong and the people with the enemy. . . . Herein lies his tragedy.

The party document also assessed Hua Guofeng; and while it gave him due recognition for his constructive role in the smashing of the Gang and certain economic works, it criticized him for leftist thinking. Hua was branded a "Whateverist"— supporting *whatever* decisions Mao made and implementing *whatever* instructions he issued—thereby perpetuating leftist errors. Hua took part in the "Anti-Deng" campaign, and after becoming party chairman blocked moves to correct the wronged cases, including the rehabilitation of victimized cadres and the Tian An Men Square Incident. He even practiced "personality cult." Worse, at the August 1977 Eleventh Central

Committee meetings he obstructed attempts to assess the Cultural Revolution critically and instead used his influence to affirm it; later he was also responsible for proceeding with hasty, leftist economic policies. The document concluded: "Obviously, for him to lead the party in correcting the leftist errors, and particularly in reestablishing the fine tradition of the party, is an impossibility."[21]

A terse and crisp assessment of Mao was made by Chairman Hu in his first major address celebrating the sixtieth anniversary of the founding of the party (July 1, 1981). Where General Huang's assessment and the party document had eulogized Mao's accomplishments from 1927 to 1949, Hu's praised the 1911 Revolution and highlighted the "Four Great People's Revolutionary Wars," which included the Northern Expedition (1926–27), the land revolution, the Japanese War (1937–45), and the War of Liberation. It appears that Hu was making a special effort to conciliate the Nationalists by tactfully implying their role in the Northern Expedition and the Japanese War.

After the establishment of the People's Republic, Hu announced, the party led the people in defeating imperialism, hegemonism, and various attempts to destroy the independence and security of the country, and achieved national unification with the exception of Taiwan and several small islands. The elimination of an exploitative class system from a country of one quarter of humanity signified a dramatic social revolution for China and an international victory for Marxism.

Mao's greatest contribution, Hu stated, was his early rejection of the "childish sickness" of worshipping foreign (Soviet) experience in the 1920s and 1930s. He creatively integrated Marxist universal principles with concrete Chinese revolutionary conditions to form a new synthesis that suited the Chinese situation. The Thought of Mao is the "crystallization of the collective wisdom of the party and a record of the victories of the great struggles of the Chinese people," and its creativeness has enriched the storehouse of Marxism. As such, Hu said, it was, is, and shall be the guiding principle of the party. Having complimented Mao, Hu then made the official criticism:

> Comrade Mao, like many great historical figures of the past, was not free from shortcomings and mistakes. The principal shortcoming occurred during his later years when, due to long and ardent support by the party and by all the people, he became smug and increasingly and seriously lost contact with realities and the masses. He separated himself from the collective leadership of the party, often rejecting or even suppressing the correct views of others. Mistakes thus became inevitable. A long period of comprehensive, serious mistakes led to the outbreak of the "Great Cultural Revolution," which brought the most severe misfortune to the party and the people. Of course, we must admit that neither before nor after the outbreak of the "Great Cultural Revolution" was the party able to prevent and turn Comrade Mao from his mistakes. On the contrary, it accepted and approved some of his erroneous proposals. We who are long-time comrades-in-arms with Comrade Mao, his long-time followers and students, must realize deeply our own responsibility and resolutely accept the necessary lessons.
>
> Nonetheless, though Comrade Mao committed serious errors in his late years, it is clear that from the perspective of his entire life his contributions to the Chinese revolution far outweigh his mistakes. . . . He was both a party founder and the principal creator of the glorious People's Liberation Army. After the establishment of the People's Republic under the leadership of the party center and Comrade Mao, China was able to stand on its feet and pioneer the socialist cause. Even when he was making serious mistakes during his last years, Comrade Mao still vigilantly guarded the independence and security of the motherland, correctly assessed new developments in world politics and led the party and the people to resist all the pressures of hegemonism, opening a new direction for our foreign relations. During the long period of struggle, all party members absorbed wisdom and strength from Comrade Mao and his thought. They nurtured the successive generations of our leaders and cadres, and educated our people of different nationalities. Comrade Mao was a great

Marxist, a great proletarian revolutionary, theorist, strategist, and the greatest national hero in Chinese history. He made immense contributions to the liberation of all oppressed peoples of the world and to human progress. His great contributions are immortal.[22]

Since Hu's speech commemorated the party's sixtieth anniversary, he appropriately praised other outstanding leaders: Zhou Enlai, Liu Shaoqi, Zhu De, Peng Dehuai, and earlier figures such as Li Dazhao, Qu Qiubai, and Li Lisan along with a number of intellectuals, scientists, two Nationalist generals who joined the Communist cause, and several foreign friends.

It is noteworthy that in the entire speech Hu never once referred to Mao as chairman but only as comrade. The "Great Cultural Revolution" was mentioned in quotes, implying his refusal to recognize its legality. The praise of Liu Shaoqi, Peng Dehuai, and Li Lisan, all Mao's enemies, revealed what the present leadership really thinks of Mao.

A Historian's View

In an objective assessment of Mao, historians who seek truth from facts will be among the first to recognize Mao's greatness as a revolutionary leader, founder of the People's Republic, and pioneer of the socialist cause in China. But they would be remiss if they overlooked his various policy blunders and their consequences. First and foremost was his rejection of any population control. Experts, including Beijing University President Ma Yinchu,[23] warned of the serious economic and social consequences of a population explosion, but Mao argued that population problems existed only in capitalist societies. The Soviet Union had no population control and did not suffer any negative consequences—why should China be different? Mao dismissed Malthusian population theories in the naïve belief that more people could do more work—more work meant more production and faster economic development. The result was an uncontrolled increase in population from 500 million in the early 1950s to nearly a billion today, while arable land, rather than increasing, actually decreased due to national disasters, increased industrial use of land, and the removal of trees for fuel by the poor.

The task of feeding, clothing, and providing shelter and employment for a billion people is a gigantic burden which no other country on earth faces. It drains much of the national resources which otherwise could be used for economic development. With 80 percent of the huge population based in the countryside, improvement of agricultural production is basic to China's socialist construction. Yet Mao followed the Soviet model of investing heavily in heavy industry and lightly in agriculture, resulting in extremely low agricultural productivity. Mao did not heed the Marxist dictum that the foundation of a society lies in the agricultural laborer's productive rate exceeding the individual needs of the laborer, creating a surplus to support the other sectors of the state. For thirty years, China's agricultural sector was neglected and semi-independent, necessitating the importation of food to meet domestic needs, and thereby consuming a considerable amount of scarce foreign exchange reserves. In 1978–79 per farm capita production amounted to only $50 a year—pitifully below any surplus that might support economic growth and improve the standard of living. Unless agricultural conditions are vastly improved and birth control is strictly enforced, China's march toward modernization will, at best, be slow and labored. In retrospect, Mao's population and agricultural policies have created the most serious obstacle to rapid modernization.

The second major policy blunder was the enforced isolation of the country. Except for the 1950s when Sino-Soviet cooperation was in full swing, China had been virtually cut off from the outside world for twenty years. Under the ideology of self-reliance Chinese science, technology, arts, education, and other aspects of culture were deprived of the benefits of developments in other countries. It was exactly during the decades of the sixties and seventies that phenomenal progress was made in the West and Japan, while China preoccupied itself with civil strife and class struggle. The cost of this isolation to China is practically incalculable.

The third policy blunder was "leftist blind actionism" and "adventurism" in economic development. At a central work conference in December 1980, party Vice-Chairman Chen Yun, an economist, pointedly declared: "Since the founding of the People's Republic, the main mistake in economic development was 'leftism.' The situation before 1957 was relatively good, but after 1958 'leftist' mistakes became increasingly serious. It was a principal mistake . . . and the main source of that mistake was leftist leadership thinking."[24] An obvious manifestation of this "wrong thinking" was an overfondness for quick results, in total disregard of objective economic realities, which resulted in "taking fantasy as truth, working stubbornly according to self-will, and carrying out work today that might be possible for the future." Such "leftist adventurism" severely under-mined the productive relations in the economic structure. Furthermore, the doctrine of uninterrupted revolution led to reckless "blind actionism" which set up unrealistic economic targets supported by a level of investment that far exceeded the country's ability to pay. What followed was an unending flow of falsified figures to deceive the leadership, and the twin evils of adventurism and blind actionism together drove the people to the brink of bankruptcy.[25]

Although knowledgeable persons recognized the irrationality of these policies, in speaking out they risked being branded as anti-Maoist or antirevolutionary—therefore the country was thrust unrestrained into one economic crisis after another. Three of the most obvious crises were: (1) the Great Leap (1958–60) which caused a loss of $66 billion and widespread starvation; (2) the disastrous Cultural Revolution (1966–76) which saw investment reach a dangerous 33 percent of the national income in 1970, resulting in government deficits for three years thereafter and an economic dislocation which threatened total collapse; and (3) the grandiose Ten-Year plan of 1976–85, which allocated to construction projects 31.1

to 36.6 percent of the national income in 1976–78, rates which came close to those of the catastrophic years of the Great Leap. Chen Yun concluded that these mistakes occurred because "our thought and action lost contact with the basic conditions of China."[26]

Mao's fourth major mistake was his assumption of an unquestionable superiority within the party, destroying party democracy and collective leadership, and opening the way for "one-man rule." As the revolutionary leader and founding father of the People's Republic, Mao endowed himself with the status of a patriarch (*jia zhang* 家長), tolerating no opinion except his own (*yi yan tang* 一言堂). His actions reflected the feudalistic notion that he who conquered the country controlled it as a family possession (*jia tian xia* 家天下). Thus, official documents frequently started with the phrase "the Chairman, and the party center . . .," suggesting one man towering above the party, mocking the collective leadership affirmed in the Eighth Party Congress. Sycophants such as secret service head Kang Sheng whetted Mao's appetite by asserting that a party history mentioning the contributions of other leaders belittled Mao and created a rival center. Thus, the party history became a chronicle of the Leader's continuous feuds with others until, one by one, he had knocked them all down.[27] Like the emperors of the past, Mao was a patriarch, Helmsman, and even god-hero, who could do no wrong. He acted with total impunity in "designating" his successor and sponsoring the rise of his wife far beyond her worth. It appears the Actonian dictum "power corrupts and absolute power corrupts absolutely" holds true even in a dictatorship of the proletariat!

In addition to granting him absolute control, Mao's political style became an example for party secretaries in the provinces and districts to follow; they behaved like small patriarchs and smaller patriarchs in their respective jurisdictions. Nothing could be done without their approval, establishing a highly bureaucratic and privileged class throughout the country.[28]

How could the party allow all this to happen? The Chinese

themselves were hard put to find a proper explanation but finally came up with two interpretations. The first states that in China, as in other communist countries, the leader of the revolutionary party was empowered with great discretionary authority and freedom of action during the seizure of power. Once success was achieved, the concentration of power had a tendency to become a tradition; and due to the obviously great contributions of the leader, his followers readily accepted his exalted status. His status eventually became institutionalized, and he received lifelong tenure as *the* Leader, as well as credit for the fruits of others' labor.

The broader official explanation concerns the profound impact of China's feudal past on the thought and action of all. The vestiges of the distinction between high and low, of the rank and grade system, and the role of the family head can be seen everywhere. Farmers and small producers were unaccustomed to controlling their own fates, relying instead on the graces of the emperor as "savior," giving in return their loyalty and gratitude. Thus, there was a powerful social precedent for the high concentration of authority in one man. Even the party itself reflected this feudal influence, permitting the emergence of a situation in which no one dared criticize the patriarch. Consequently, collective leadership and democratic centralism became meaningless: in the former, one was "more equal" than others, and in the latter, centralism prevailed over democracy.[29]

These explanations are certainly valid, but they omit one key element: it was Mao's firm control of the army, the secret police, the security apparatus, the 8341 unit, and the network of intelligence and investigatory agencies, which made opposition to him virtually impossible. Those who dared to criticize him risked their futures and even their lives.

In conclusion, historians will agree that Mao was supremely successful as a revolutionary but extremely erratic as a nation builder. His great achievements before 1957 may serve as an inspiration to others, but his major mistakes thereafter must serve as a lesson to all.

A NEW LEADERSHIP AND A NEW ORDER

With the delicate assessment of Mao finally out of the way and the party's guilt recognized, a heavy psychological burden was lifted. The new power structure put Hu, Deng, and Zhao firmly in control of the party, the military, and the government, and cemented their plans for China's future. They are committed to a revolution of modernization. Lest there be any misunderstanding, Hu impressed upon the nation the following six points in his speech commemorating the sixtieth anniversary of the founding of the party:[30]

1. All party members must dedicate themselves to modern construction of Chinese socialism regardless of personal sacrifice, and serve the people with all their hearts and minds.

2. Under the new historical conditions, we must advance Marxism and the Thought of Mao Zedong. [Hu reaffirmed the importance of the four basic principles: the socialist line, the proletarian dictatorship, the leadership of the Communist Party, and Marxism-Leninism and the Thought of Mao.]

3. We must further strengthen the democratic life of the party and tighten the party discipline. . . . We must forbid any form of individual worship. . . . All important issues must be decided after collective discussions by appropriate party committees. No one man should have the final say. All members of the committees involved must abide by such decisions. At all levels of party organization, we must implement collective leadership . . . with emphasis on quality and efficiency. [To enhance party democracy,] any member has the right to criticize party leaders at party meetings, even including the top leaders at the center, with impunity. [But no one is allowed to create his own independent kingdom.]

4. We must regularly dust ourselves off in order to insure revolutionary youthfulness permanently within the political framework of the government. [Very pointedly Hu admitted] in the past excessive struggles resulted in a counter-

productive situation in which no one dared to make self-criticism or offer criticism. We must rectify this unhealthy style of behavior.

5. We must select young and vigorous cadres of character and knowledge for different levels of leadership.

6. We must persist in supporting internationalism and share the breathings and the lives of the proletarian class and people all over the world. . . . In dealing with strong and rich countries we must preserve our national dignity and independence, never permitting any cowering or toadying action and thought. We must be determined to unite all people including those on Taiwan in the sacred struggle for the return of Taiwan to the motherland.

It is clear that Mao's political work style and approach to economic development would not be followed: there would be no more personal worship, no suppression of free expression in party meetings, and no penalty for criticizing the leaders. However, all cadres were to be subordinated to orders from above to carry out economic construction, without feigning compliance while secretly resisting implementation. Also rejected were Maoist ideas of class struggle, disdain for intellectuals and foreign contacts, and opposition to limited private enterprise.

To ensure the success of socialist modernization, which is "a great revolution in itself," Hu called for intraparty and party-citizen unity as well as international exchanges in economics, culture, and science and technology, in order to develop a "prosperous, strong, highly democratic, and highly cultured modern socialist power," which will ultimately lead China to the communist utopia.

Hu's speech, together with the communiqué and resolution of the Sixth Plenum, was a crowning testimony to the victory of the pragmatists. In the spirit of unity, stability, conciliation, pragmatism, democracy, and realistic economic development, a new order was born under new historical conditions. With this, the Maoist era has come to an end.

From the perspective of China's long history, every sixty years formed a cycle, and the history of the Chinese Communist Party seems to be no exception. The monumental changes now unfolding are a promising sign of the nation's viability, and the people of China welcome the beginning of a new age with rising expectations.

CHINESE COMMUNISM: A THIRTY-YEAR REVIEW

On October 1, 1949, standing atop the Gate of Heavenly Peace to proclaim the establishment of the People's Republic, Mao shouted triumphantly: "The Chinese people have stood up!" What a heroic voice, what an auspicious beginning! Foreign imperialism and domestic opposition had been swept away, and the country was unified in a way unknown since the mid-nineteenth century. China was a blank canvas for the artist Mao; and his revolutionary romanticism, vision, idealism, and egalitarianism had caught the imagination of millions inside and outside China. The charismatic leader's articulation of a national purpose and the promise of the future reinforced the desire of 500 million people to rebuild their country. The galaxy of talents surrounding Mao and contributing to the success of the revolution seemed to ensure China's goals of domestic security, international respectability, and eventual emergence as a great world power.

That these goals have been met at least in part is obvious. The greatest accomplishments have been the unification of China (except Taiwan) under one central government, the attainment of the status of a major participant in world affairs, the elimination of the curse of landlordism, the laying of a foundation for industrialization, the improvement of public health, the selective development of science and technology (especially in nuclear power and rocketry), the improvement of literacy, and significant archeological finds that may result in new interpretations of ancient Chinese history. The provision of subsistence-level food, housing, clothing, and employment for nearly a billion people answers a challenge no other country on earth has ever had to meet. Finally, statistics show considerable increases in total industrial and agricultural productions and in social services.

Yet, recent Chinese leaders have openly acknowledged that despite selective progress, the country remains in a state of dire poverty and scarcity (*yi qiong er bai*). The physical complexion of the country and the livelihood of the people have not substantially changed in twenty years;[31] the gap between China and advanced countries is probably wider today than in 1949 due to phenomenal progress in science, technology, and economic development in other countries. What is it that keeps China from making greater progress in the three decades following liberation?

The chief deterrents within China have been political instability and the destruction of the principle of democracy within and without the party. Except for seven years (1949–56) of revolutionary momentum and the euphoria of building a new order, China's recent history has been plagued with such upheaval and strife that the country has been nearly destroyed. Political turmoil has resulted in the loss of much able talent, interruptions in economic development, and devastation of intellectual and artistic creativity.

In considering the source of Chinese political instability, the Eighth Party Congress of 1956 is generally viewed as the Rubicon in political development. This Congress, like the previous one, stressed party democracy and free discussion of issues. The Second Plenum of the Seventh Congress had explicitly enjoined the development of a "personality cult" by forbidding the glorification of leaders through literature, birthday celebrations, or renaming cities and streets after them. Throughout the Seventh Congress (1949–56) participants expressed their views freely, creating what might be called "A Hall of Many Voices" (*Qun yan tang*). Party democracy and collective wisdom seemed to assure the new nation's progress.

The Eighth Congress likewise stressed collective leadership and a democratic style of work, while opposing bureaucratism and worship of the individual, characteristics already apparent in the party hierarchy. Liu Shaoqi delivered the keynote report which enumerated the great successes of Chinese socialism in eliminating former class conflicts.[32] In view of these socialist transformations, Liu maintained that the conflict between the capitalist and proletarian classes had been largely resolved, and current contradictions existed only between the productive forces of advanced socialism and those of "backward" socialism. The Congress resolved that henceforth the focal point of the party and the government should be "the transformation of our country from a backward agricultural state to an advanced industrial state as fast as possible." It called for the modernization of industry, agriculture, communications, and national defense. While science and technology were not specified, they were recognized as basic to all other development. The Congress reflected China's bright future under the collective leadership of Mao, Liu, Zhou, and Zhu De; and the period from 1956 to early 1957 was regarded as a "springtime" in party history.

Into this springtime Mao introduced the Hundred Flowers Campaign. When intellectuals criticized sharply certain party policies, Mao responded as though Chinese communism itself were endangered by the criticism, and launched the Antirightist Campaign which adversely affected as many as one million people. Mao overthrew the decisions of the Eighth Congress, proclaiming that "the decisions of the Eighth Party Congress referring to the major contradiction between the productive forces of advanced and backward socialism is incorrect," and that capitalist-proletarian class conflict and capitalist-socialist line struggle remained the principal contradictions in Chinese society. From then on Mao enlarged the scope of class struggle which caused ceaseless turmoil. Rejecting collective leadership, the concept of patriarchal rule gained ascendancy and the party center became "The Hall of One Voice" (*Yi yan tang*). When Defense Minister Peng Dehuai expressed his views on the Great Leap in 1959, he was dismissed and disgraced as a "rightist opportunist." Thereafter, no one dared speak out. Party democracy was shattered, and the tenets of the Eighth Congress were negated.[33]

Once Mao's "omnipotence" was demonstrated, opportunists

and intriguers crowded around him, gaining power by controlling access to him. Their power struggles reverberated throughout the nation in intensified class struggle and in the Cultural Revolution. The dominance of Kang Sheng, Lin Biao, and the Gang of Four turned the proletarian dictatorship into a fascist one, with the added features of feudalism and revisionism.[34]

Political instability and the disappearance of party democracy inevitably affected economic development and the people's lives. On July 1, 1979, an editorial in the *People's Daily* commented:

> In the past thirty years whenever party democracy was relatively sufficient and democratic centralism relatively healthy, party leadership in economic work was in tune with reality. When problems arose, they were discovered and corrected easily, bringing about rapid socialist economic development. Whenever there was a lack of democracy in the party, nobody dared to speak out or speak the truth. Blind obedience was prevalent and the party's economic policies frequently lost touch with reality and objective laws. Socialist economic development then slowed, stagnated, or even retrogressed.[35]

Chinese statistics show that economic development was marked by three short periods of growth (1949–57, 1963–65, 1977–79) and two longer periods of decline (1958–62, 1966–76). During Mao's twenty-seven-year rule, only 1952–57 were years of genuine growth, while 1949–52 represented a recovery from the civil war and 1963–65 a recovery from the Great Leap. The period 1977–79 was a recovery from the Cultural Revolution as well as a response to the death of Mao and the fall of the Gang. The following statistics summarize development in the past thirty years.

China's erratic development demonstrates that revolutionary leaders who were skillful in political struggle were not necessarily knowledgeable in economic matters. Mao in particular would not heed the advice of economic experts or act according to economic laws and the realities of the country. In the fifties he adopted the Soviet model for development and emphasized

PERIODS OF RECOVERY AND GROWTH

	1949–52	1953–57	1963–65	1977	1978
Industry	36%	19.2%	7.9%	14.1%	13.5%
Agriculture	14%	4.5%	11.1%		
National Income	n.a.	n.a.	14.5%		

PERIODS OF DECLINE

	1958–62	1967	1968	1974	1976
Industry	+3.8%	−13.8%	−5%	+0.3%	+1.3%
Agriculture	−4.3%		−2.5%		
National Income	−3.9%				

(Figures from the *Journal of Philosophy and Social Sciences,* Nanjing University, No. 3:1–8, 1979.

heavy industry over agriculture and light industry, when the concrete situation in China suggested the reverse as more logical. When the Soviet model proved ill-suited, he precipitously resorted to the Commune and the Great Leap. What followed for more than a decade was the familiar saga of "leftist adventurism," which caused such waste of time, energy, capital, and valuable talents. Consequently, Chinese per capita income today ranks last among the socialist countries, and productivity lags behind that of Hong Kong and South Korea.[36]

Yet, in spite of political instability and erratic economic development, progress was registered as indicated in the following table. For the purpose of comparison, three sets of figures are given for each entry whenever possible: from an official American source, an official Chinese source, and an independent scholar (W. Klatt).

These figures reveal a substantial growth frequently obscured by the larger picture of political and social upheaval. Between 1952 and 1977 the GNP grew 4.5 times, industrial development averaged a 9 percent annual growth rate, and agricultural, a 2 percent rate of growth.[37] Under a stable political leadership with realistic economic policies, the record would have been far more impressive. The population explosion and the diversion of funds to industrial development

	1952	1957	1977	1978	1979	1980
Population (million)						
CIA	570	640	987	1,001	1,018	
Chinese	574.8	646.5	945.2	958.1	970.92	982.22
GNP						
Independent (1952 = 100)	100	140	510	573	597	627
CIA (billion 1978 US$)	99	138	398	444	468	
Per capita GNP						
CIA (1978 US$)	174	216	403	439	460	
Chinese	43.3	59.1			230	
Independent					300	
Agricultural production						
Independent (1952 = 100)	100	111	277	302	327	335
CIA (1957 = 100)	84	100	146	151		
Grain (including soy beans)						
CIA (million metric tons)	161	191	283	305	315	318
Chinese	163.9	195	283	305	332	
Independent	164	195	282.7	304	312.5	(−4.2%)

	1952	1957	1977	1978	1979	1980
Cotton (mmt)						
CIA	1.3	1.6	2	2.2	2.2	
Chinese		1.64	2.04	2.16	2.2	(+22.7%)
Independent	1.3	1.6	2	2.2	2.4	
Industrial production						
Independent (1952 = 100)	100	206	1,087	1,234	1,340	1,420
CIA (1957 = 100)	48	100	574	651	703	
Coal (mmt)						
CIA	66.5	130.7	550	618	625	620 (−2.4%)
Chinese	66.4	131	550	618	635	
Independent	66.5	130.7	550	618	620	
Crude Steel (mmt)						
CIA	1.3	5.4	23.7	31.8	34.0	37.12 (+7.7%)
Chinese	1.35	5.35	23.74	31.8	34.48	
Independent	1.3	5.3	23.70	31.8	32.0	
Crude Oil (mmt)						
CIA	0.4	1.5	90.3	100.3	106.15	105.95 (−.2%)
Chinese	0.44	1.46	93.64	104.1	110.0	
Independent	0.4	1.5	93.6	104.0		
Electric Power (billion kwh)						
CIA	7.3	19.3	141.0	162.0	281.95	300.6 (+6.6%)
Chinese	7.3	19.3	223.4	256.6	281.95	
Independent	7.3	19.3	223.4	256.5	275.0	

Foreign Trade
(billion current US$)

Exports

CIA	.9	1.6	8.1	9.9	13.0	
Chinese	.94	2.2	9.0	10.7	12.4	17.9 (+28.7%)
Independent			9.0	11.2	14.1	

Imports

CIA	1	1.4	7.1	11.2	14.7	
Chinese	1.3	2	8.5	11.9	16.0	19.2 (+19.2%)
Independent			8.6	12.5	16.2	

Sources: National Foreign Assessment Center, Central Intelligence Agency, *China: Economic Indicators* (Dec. 1978); *China: In Pursuit of Modernization* (Dec. 1978); *China: A Statistical Compendium* (July 1979); *China: The Continuing Search for a Modernization Strategy* (April 1980); W. Klatt, "China's New Economic Policy: A Statistical Appraisal," *The China Quarterly*, 80:716–33, Dec. 1979; Chinese Statistics Updated," *The China Quarterly*, 84:737–43, Dec. 1980; "Communiqué on Fulfillment of China's 1980 National Economic Plan," issued on April 29, 1981, by the State Statistical Bureau, *Beijing Review*, 19:23–27, May 11, 1981; 20:17–20, May 18, 1981; Chinese State Statistical Bureau, "1949–1979 Economic and Statistical Data, Selected Compilation," in *Zhongguo jinji niankan* (Annual economic report of China), overseas Chinese edition (Hong Kong, 1981), VI, 3–31.

that should have been allocated for the improvement of people's livelihood resulted in an extremely low standard of living and a concomitant loss of work enthusiasm and entrepreneurial spirit. The burden of the rapid development of heavy industry was carried by farmers (80 percent of the population), who at best subsisted precariously.

It is heartening that recent innovations have somewhat relieved the plight of the peasants. The government has allowed them to keep produce above the assigned quotas, operate private plots (5–20 percent of the land), engage in sideline handicrafts, and sell their products in the free market. In 1980 certain selected areas went so far as to parcel out communal land to individual households for cultivation. Work enthusiasm returned overnight and productivity rose at once. The communes in these areas, though not officially dissolved, now exist in name only. These changes indicate the present leadership's sensitivity to past mistakes.

Indeed, the lessons to be learned from the past thirty years are many. First and foremost, there must be political and social stability to enable the government to carry out orderly reform and development. Second, population control must be strictly enforced so as to achieve a zero growth rate. Third, international cooperation must be strengthened in all areas including science, technology, education, and the arts. Fourth, war must be avoided if possible for it is the biggest waster of financial and human resources. Fifth, the political system must be reformed to prevent the recurrence of patriarchal rule and to ensure democracy within and without the party.[38] Bureaucratism, lifelong tenure of cadres, and special privileges should be reduced (if not eliminated), with the institution of a benevolent retirement system. Sixth, economic development must be neither "leftist" nor "rightist" but "centrist," based on realities and economic laws. China must recognize that there is no shortcut to wealth and power and be prepared for gradual development under expert guidance, expecting only a moderate but steady progress (*xiao kang*).[39] Last but not least, the traditional diligence of the Chinese people must be revived, their work enthusiasm rekindled, and their creativity encouraged. Liberating the potential of a billion people and providing opportunities for their self-fulfillment could result in an explosion of learning, production, and creative accomplishment such as the world has never seen.

While such changes will be difficult to institute, it is imperative that China move in these directions. Chinese leaders themselves have recognized the need for reform and avoiding previous mistakes. While much correction has already begun, much remains to be accomplished. With a steady hand at the helm of the ship of state, China will move forward slowly but surely. Whether it can be counted in the front ranks of world powers by the year 2000 is questionable, but in time the Chinese people will undoubtedly exert themselves and transform their country into one that is both thoroughly modern and distinctly Chinese.

NOTES

1. *Central Daily News,* Nov. 16, 1980. Based on Nationalist intelligence reports.
2. *Ibid.,* Aug. 12, 1980. Intelligence reports.
3. *Ibid.,* Jan. 29, 1981. Intelligence reports.
4. *The Christian Science Monitor,* Jan. 16, 1981.
5. Including the famous sociologist Fei Xiaotong.
6. The five generals were: Huang Yongsheng, 70, former chief-of-staff of the Liberation Army; Wu Faxian, 65, former air force commander; Li Zuopeng, 66, former political commissar for the Navy; Qiu Huizuo, 66, former head of the army logistics department; and Jiang Tengjiao, 61, former air force commander in Nanjing.
7. Full text of indictment in *A Great Trial in Chinese History* (Beijing, 1981), pp. 18–26, 148–49.
8. The coal minister was Zhang Linzhi. Eleven professors and acquaintances of Liu Shaoqi were tortured and three of them died. See *A Great Trial,* pp. 43–45, 56–57.
9. *A Great Trial,* p. 39.
10. *Central Daily News,* Dec. 13, 1980.
11. *The Christian Science Monitor,* Dec. 30, 1980.

12. *A Great Trial*, p. 105.
13. *Central Daily News*, Jan. 11 and 12, 1981. Nationalist intelligence reports.
14. Interview by a University of California student, Mark Dowie, "China's Differing Moods on the Gang of Four," *Daily Nexus*, Jan. 8, 1981.
15. *Ibid.*
16. *Time* Magazine, Jan. 12, 1981, p. 28.
17. *The Christian Science Monitor*, Dec. 18, 1980.
18. Full text of Huang's speech in the *Renmin Ribao* [People's daily], April 11, 1981. Tr. in quotes are mine. There is an abridged version of English translation in *Beijing Review*, No. 17, April 17, 1981.
19. Remarks by Vice-Chairman Chen Yun in the *Renmin Ribao* [People's daily], April 9, 1981.
20. "Communiqué of the Sixth Plenary Session of the 11th Central Committee of CPC," adopted June 29, 1981, *Beijing Review*, No. 27, July 6, 1981, pp. 6–9.
21. Chinese text of the "Resolution" in the *Renmin Ribao* [People's daily], July 1, 1981. Tr. mine. An English version, somewhat less literal than mine, may be found in *Beijing Review*, No. 27, July 6, 1981, pp. 10–39.
22. Chinese text of Hu's speech in the *Renmin Ribao* [People's daily], July 2, 1981. Tr. mine.
23. And others such as Chen Da and Wu Jingchao.
24. "Leadership Thinking in Rectifying Economic Work: On the Leftist Mistakes in Economic Construction," by a special commentator of the *Renmin Ribao* [People's daily]. Chinese text in *Renmin Ribao*, April 9, 1981. Tr. mine.
25. *Ibid.*
26. *Ibid.*
27. *Renmin Ribao*, Sept. 18, 1980, p. 5.
28. "On the Necessity of Reforming the Leadership System," by a commentator of the *Hongqi* [Red flag] Magazine. Chinese text in *Hongqi*, No. 17, 1980, pp. 2–4.
29. *Ibid.*, pp. 5–8.
30. Full text in the *Renmin Ribao* [People's daily], July 2, 1981. Tr. mine.
31. According to Hu Qiaomu, president of the Chinese Academy of Social Sciences. See his article, "Observe Economic Laws, Speed Up the Four Modernizations," *Peking Review*, No. 47, Nov. 24, 1978, pp. 18–19.
32. 1. Elimination of bureaucratic-comprador-capitalist class.
    2. Liquidation of landlord class and disappearance of rich peasants.

3. Transformation of bourgeoisie class from exploiter to workers.
4. Transformation of individual peasants and workers into collective workers.
5. Working class assuming leadership positions.
6. The reform of intellectualism to serve socialism.
33. Lu Zhongjian, "Sanshi nian di jiaoxun" (The lessons of thirty years), *Zhengming* Magazine, Hong Kong, No. 24, Oct. 1, 1979, pp. 8, 11.
34. *Ibid.*, 14.
35. *Renmin Ribao*, [People's daily], July 1, 1979. Tr. mine.
36. Lu Zhongjian, p. 6.
37. National Assessment Center, *China: In Pursuit of Economic Modernization* (Washington, D.C., 1978), p. 1.
38. *Hongqi* [Red flag], No. 17, 1980, pp. 2–4.
39. *Renmin Ribao* [People's daily], April 9, 1981.

FURTHER READING

A Great Trial in Chinese History (Beijing, 1981).

"Aiguo zhuyi shi jianshe shehui zhuyi di juda jingshen liliang" (Patriotism is a great spiritual power in building socialism), *Renmin Ribao* [People's daily], March 19, 1981.

"Communiqué on Fulfillment of China's 1980 National Economic Plan," issued on April 29, 1981, by the State Statistical Bureau, *Beijing Review*, 19:23–27 (May 11, 1981); 20:17–20 (May 18, 1981).

"Communiqué of the Sixth Plenary Session of the 11th Central Committee of CPC," adopted on June 29, 1981, *Beijing Review*, 27:6–8 (July 6, 1981).

"Comrade Ye Jianying's Speech—At the Meeting in Celebration of the 30th Anniversary of the Founding of the People's Republic of China," *Beijing Review*, 40:7–32 (Oct. 5, 1979). Complete Chinese text in *Renmin Ribao* [People's daily], Sept. 30, 1979.

"Duanzheng jinji gongzuo di zhidao sixiang: Lun jinji jianshe zhong di zuoqing cuowu" (The leadership's thinking in rectifying economic work: On the leftist mistakes in economic construction), *Renmin Ribao* [People's daily], Peking, April 9, 1981.

Han, Suyin, *Wind in the Tower: Mao Tse-tung and the Chinese Revolution, 1949–1975* (Boston, 1976).

Hu Yaobang, "Speech Commemorating the 60th Anniversary of the Founding of the Chinese Communist Party," Chinese text

in the *Renmin Ribao* [People's daily], July 2, 1981; English
tr. in *Beijing Review*, 28:9–24 (July 13, 1981).

Huang, Kecheng, "How to Assess Chairman Mao and Mao Zedong
Thought," *Beijing Review*, 17:15–23 (April 27, 1981).

Johnson, Chalmers, "The Failure of Socialism in China," *Issues &
Studies*, XV:7:22–33 (July 1979).

Kallgren, Joyce K. (ed.), *The People's Republic of China after
Thirty Years: An Overview* (Berkeley, 1979).

Li, Honglin, "Kexue he mixin" (Science and superstition), *Renmin
Ribao* [People's daily], Peking, Oct. 2, 1978.

———, "Chinese Communist Party Is Capable of Correcting Its
Mistakes," *Beijing Review*, 25:17–20 (June 22, 1981).

Li, Victor H., *Law without Lawyers: A Comparative View of Law
in the United States and China* (Boulder, 1978).

"Lingdao zhidu bixu gaige" (The leadership system must be reformed), *Hongqi* [Red flag], 17:2–4, (1980). Written by a
commentator of the journal.

Liu, Kwang-ching, "World View and Peasant Rebellion: Reflections
on Post-Mao Historiography," *The Journal of Asian Studies*,
XL:2:295–326 (Feb. 1981).

Lu, Zhongjian, "Sanshi nian di jiaoxun" (The lessons of thirty
years), *Zhengming* Magazine, Hong Kong, 24:5–15, (Oct. 1,
1979).

Lu, Shi, " 'Mao xuan' wujuan yingdang chongshen chongbian"
(Vol. 5 of Mao's *Selected Works* should be reexamined and
reedited), *Zhengming* Magazine, Hong Kong, 24:16–17 (Oct.
1, 1979).

Morath, Inge, and Arthur Miller, *Chinese Encounters* (New York,
1979).

Oxnam, Robert B., and Richard C. Bush (eds.), *China Briefing,
1980* (Boulder, 1980).

Pye, Lucian W., *Mao Tse-tung: The Man in the Leader* (New
York, 1976).

"Quanli buneng guofen jizhong yu geren" (Power should not be
overly concentrated in one man), *Hongqi* [Red flag], 17:5–8
(1980). Written by a special commentator of the journal believed to be one close to Vice-Chairman Deng Xiaoping.

"Resolution on Certain Questions in the History of Our Party Since
the Founding of the People's Republic of China." Adopted
June 27, 1981, at the Sixth Plenary Session of the Eleventh
Central Committee of Chinese Communist Party. Chinese text
in *Renmin Ribao* [People's daily], July 1, 1981; English translation in *Beijing Review*, 27:10–39 (July 6, 1981).

Shao, Yü-ming, "Shih-lun Chung-Kung cheng-ch'üan tsai Chung-
kuo chin-tai-shih shang ti kung-kuo" (An appraisal of the

achievements and failures of the Chinese Communist regime in modern Chinese history), *Hai-wai hsüeh-jen* [Overseas scholars], Taipei, 99:6–20 (Oct. 1980).

Wilson, Dick (ed.), *Mao Tse-tung in the Scales of History* (Cambridge, Eng., 1977).

Witke, Roxane, *Comrade Chiang Ch'ing* (Boston, 1977).

Yahuda, Michael, "Political Generations in China," *The China Quarterly*, 80:793–805 (Dec. 1979).

"Yao gongkai di kexue di ping Mao" (Mao should be openly and scientifically assessed) *Zhengming* Magazine, Hong Kong, 24:4 (Oct. 1, 1979), editorial.

6

Taiwan's "Economic Miracle" and the Prospect for Unification with Mainland China

Walking down the main streets of Taipei, one witnesses an unending flow of motorcycles, buses, and cars, with hotels, modern apartments, and high-rise office buildings on each side. Inside the office is the controlled chaos of successful enterprise; the electronic chorus of elevators, air conditioners, typewriters, and computers is punctuated by the ringing of telephones and the raised voices of those making overseas calls. Farmers a world away from Taipei's bustle proudly show the fruits of their labor; nicely clothed and fed, with modest but comfortable homes, they appear content with their lives.

This is modern Taiwan, transformed from an agricultural society to an industrial power within a generation. The title "Little Japan" evokes a mixed reaction of open displeasure and secret pride. In East Asia, Taiwan is indeed second only to Japan in terms of industrialization, foreign trade, and quality of life. Taiwan's success is its most important weapon in the struggle for survival, security, and international ties. A close look at Taiwan's accomplishments will help explain its current position and future course.

Taiwan has enjoyed peace, stability, and sustained economic

growth for thirty years. The economic growth rate averaged 7.3 percent per annum in the 1950s, 9.1 percent in the 1960s, and 11.9 percent from 1971–73. The recession of 1974–75 affected Taiwan severely, but by 1978 growth had reached a peak of 12.8 percent. In 1979 and 1980 the rate of growth leveled off to 8.08 and 6.7 percent respectively. The growth in foreign trade has been most spectacular, reaching $39.48 billion in 1980 and generating a surplus of $46.5 million. In 1980 Taiwan boasted of a GNP of $40.3 billion and a per capita GNP of $2,100, and of a gold and foreign exchange reserve of $7.4 billion. In three decades the GNP has increased 1,000 percent, and the targets of the New Ten-Year Plan (1981–89) call for a GNP of $69.1 billion in 1989 with a per capita income of $6,017.[1] With the achievement of these goals, Taiwan will be counted among the developed areas of the world.

It is most noteworthy that wealth has not been concentrated in a few hands but is shared by a majority of people, in fulfillment of the ancient ideal of an "equitable distribution of wealth" (*ch'ün-fu* 均 富). The income ratio of the highest and lowest 20 percent of wage earners in 1952 was 15:1; but in 1964 only 5.33:1; and by 1978, 4.18:1, less of a gap than the United States.[2] Televisions, refrigerators, washing machines, and telephones have become common, while unemployment is kept below 2 percent. The average lifespan for man is sixty-nine, and woman, seventy-four, and the daily intake of calories is 2,845 and protein, 80 grams, both exceeding international standards. Almost unique in the simultaneous attainment of rapid economic growth and the equitable distribution of wealth, one can say that Taiwan today probably enjoys the highest standard of living in Chinese history.

CAUSES OF TAIWAN'S ECONOMIC SUCCESS

Economic Strategy

Taiwan's economic strategy has given priority to agriculture, light industry, and heavy industry in descending order. From

1949 to 1960, the thrust of policy was toward development of agriculture and light industry, beginning with a three-stage land reform program and followed by labor and technological innovations that accelerated farm production. Measures were also taken to expand the physical and social infrastructure, to stabilize prices, to reform the foreign exchange system, and to develop light, import-replacement industries.

Small and resource-poor, Taiwan had no choice but to depend on trade. Recognizing this, the economic planners emphasized industrialization and exports in the 1960s. Measures were adopted to increase the production of durable consumer goods (light industry), encourage labor-intensive, export-oriented assembly industries, and diversify agricultural products for export. Electronics, synthetic fiber, and plastics industries grew rapidly and moved into the world market. With labor costs low and quality control high, Taiwan's products competed successfully in foreign markets.

In the 1970s the emphasis was shifted to developing sophisticated and heavy industry as well as to expanding the infrastructure. In 1973 ten major projects (seven of them infrastructure related) was launched at a cost of $7 billion: (1) the North-South Freeway known as the Sun Yat-sen Memorial Express Way; (2) the international airport at Taoyuan outside Taipei named after Chiang Kai-shek; (3) electrification of the west coast railway trunkline; (4) the northern coastal railway; (5) the Taichung Harbor; (6) the Suao Harbor expansion; (7) the nuclear plant at Chin-shan near the northern tip of the island with two generating units; (8) the modern steel mill called the China Steel Corporation; (9) the giant China Ship Building Corporation; and (10) a petrochemical complex. The last three are located at or near Kaohsiung, which was transformed into a special municipality in 1979 on a par with Taipei.

With the completion of these ten projects in 1979, Taiwan took on the appearance of a "rich developing nation." The projects injected a large dosage of capital into the economy and relieved the recession of 1974–75. Moreover, a large number of economic planners, engineers, and technicians working on these projects gained valuable experience, and numerous workers received training in the process, giving all a new confidence in their ability to build a modern society with their own hands.

To fully utilize these new skills and to further modernize the island, the government immediately launched the twelve new projects with emphasis on technology- and capital-intensive industries. These include expanding steel mills, adding nuclear power plants, constructing new cross-island highways, completing Taichung Harbor and the round-the-island railway system, extending the freeway, improving regional irrigation and drainage, building major sea dikes, increasing farm mechanization, and constructing new towns, cultural centers, and housing. With the successful completion of these projects Taiwan will be a "Treasure Island" among developed countries.

Means of Modernization

Modernization requires capital, qualified personnel, and scientific management. While government and domestic private investment have constituted a major source of capital, foreign and overseas Chinese (ethnic Chinese of Singapore, Hong Kong, the U.S., etc.) investments have been heavy due to Taiwan's favorable investment conditions. In 1960 the Statute for Encouragement of Investment offered a deferrable five-year income tax exemption for capital-intensive and high-technology industries. It set a maximum income tax liability of 25 percent after the tax holiday and offered other privileges such as exemptions from export taxes, customs duties, business taxes, etc. In 1979 the Statute was revised to offer tax credit to further attract foreign capital, and the substantial investments from abroad continue to grow.

The creation of three Export Processing Zones—two in Kaohsiung area and one near Taichung—in the 1960s also encouraged foreign investment by simplifying customs procedures and export regulations. By 1974 a total of $156,755,000 had been invested in 291 Export Zone projects, and exports totaled $511,322,000 with a favorable balance of over $200 million.

Introduction of new production techniques from abroad had also played an important role in rapid economic development. Under the Statute of Technical Cooperation a total of 837 cases of technical cooperation under private agreements was made between 1952 and 1974. Japan led the way with 615 cases, the United States followed with 151, while Europe accounted for 57 cases and other countries, 14.[3]

The qualified personnel that encourages investment and modernization has been provided by Taiwan's excellent educational system. A nine-year free education is available to all. By 1977–78, 99.6 percent of the elementary school age group were attending primary schools; 50.9 percent of those between fifteen and seventeen years of age were attending senior high school; and 25.2 percent of those between eighteen and twenty-one were attending the 101 colleges and universities. In addition, Taiwan has sent a large number of students to the United States for advanced studies.[4] Thus there is no shortage of trained personnel on the island.

Abundant incentives and privileges as well as trained personnel and cheap labor prompted foreign and overseas Chinese investments to grow quickly from a few million dollars each year in the 1950s to $213 million in 1978. In twenty-five years (1952–78) those investments totaled $1.92 billion—31 percent ($595 million) from overseas Chinese, 30 percent ($586 million) from the United States, 17 percent ($321 million) from Japan, and 12 percent ($227 million) from Europe. Favorite investment targets were electronic and electrical products ($633 million) and chemicals ($291 million), followed by services, machinery and instruments, metal products, and textiles.

The United States' recognition of the People's Republic of China on January 1, 1979, had little impact on economic growth and foreign investments in Taiwan. The 1979 GNP registered a 20 percent increase; foreign trade, 31 percent; and foreign investments, 50 percent. More remarkably, informal trade with mainland China via Hong Kong and Japan reached $100 million.[5] The International Monetary Fund reckoned that Taiwan's foreign trade in 1978 was the second largest in Asia and twenty-first in the world.

Foreign confidence in Taiwan's economy was demonstrated in December 1979 through a grant of $428 million in low-interest loans to China Airlines, the Taiwan Power Company, and the China Steel Corporation by a consortium of banks from ten countries including the United States, several European countries, Japan, and Singapore. Thus Taiwan's industrial modernization continues to forge ahead.

Rapid industrialization has created inevitable environmental and social problems including traffic, pollution, industrial waste, inflation, juvenile delinquency, and the migration of rural populations to urban centers swelling the cities to a full 56 percent of the island's total population.[6] The most serious social and economic problem appears to be the uncontrolled birth rate, which has resulted in an astounding population density of 497 people per square kilometer (8,159 per square kilometer in Taipei).[7] With an annual growth rate of 1.86 percent, the present population of 17.8 million will double in thirty-five years. Repeated government efforts to cut the rate to 1.25 percent per year have met with no success; new attempts are being made to raise the age of marriage, and various birth control methods are being promoted. There is no doubt that population growth must be checked if Taiwan is to continue to improve its standard of living.

Chiang Ching-kuo deserves much credit for his leadership in economic development and in weathering the storm of American rapprochement with Beijing. An efficient administrator surrounded by economic, scientific and managerial experts, he is keenly interested in economic affairs and the livelihood of the people. As premier in 1973 he initiated the ten major modernization projects, followed by the twelve more recent ones. At Chiang Kai-shek's death in 1975, Vice-President C.K. Yen succeeded as president, while the younger Chiang was elected chairman of the Nationalist Party. Yen finished his term in May 1978, and Chiang Ching-kuo, sixty-eight, was elected president for a six-year term by a nearly unanimous vote in the National Assembly.

Chiang Ching-kuo maintains an extreme filial piety to his father, but the two are quite different in training, outlook, temperament, and life style. The elder Chiang was more formal, stern, distant, and militarily oriented; the younger Chiang is more personable, approachable, and economically oriented. He visits farmers, soldiers, hospital patients, and mixes with intellectuals, artists, writers, and baseball players with equal ease. In this way he acts in the ancient tradition of "loving the people" (*ch'in-min*). He is well liked by both Taiwanese and mainlanders on Taiwan, as he symbolizes unity and economic development as well as improvement of the people's livelihood.

Thus far, Chiang's administration is characterized by political innovation, economic development, social stability and welfare, and military preparedness. He believes that the age of individual heroism is past and urges all to contribute their utmost in building a promising future. He is especially mindful of cultivating able young talent and of promoting native Taiwanese into the mainstream of government. His vice-president (Shieh Tung-ming), the governor of Taiwan, the mayor of Taipei, several cabinet ministers, and a large number of the members of the Legislative Yüan as well as of the representative assemblies are Taiwanese. Chiang's administration is exhibiting an increasing liberalism, but he steadfastly refuses to yield the Nationalist claim to jurisdiction over all of China or to negotiate with Beijing (unless it foregoes communism); nor will he tolerate the Taiwanese Independence Movement, negotiations with the Soviet Union, the propagation of communism on Taiwan, or attacks on the Nationalist party and the Three People's Principles.

While proud of its economic growth, Taiwan takes greater pride in its role of preserver of the Chinese cultural heritage. The Palace Museum holds more than 300,000 invaluable Chinese paintings, calligraphy, porcelain, jade and bronze pieces, and other art objects from the previous imperial col-

President Chiang Ching-kuo visits with the people.

lections. The people on Taiwan openly proclaim that while their island is small in size, it is economically dynamic and culturally great, and that it has the potential of becoming "a great country of tomorrow." Taiwan is determined to create a model of modern development based on free enterprise and the Three People's Principles as an alternative to the system on the mainland, and hopes that Beijing will ultimately recognize it as the way to modernization.[8]

THE PROSPECT FOR REUNIFICATION

The reunification of China is the common desire of all Chinese, Nationalist and Communist. Taiwan has openly expressed concern for the livelihood of the people on the mainland, and not a few mainlanders harbor secret admiration for the economic success of Taiwan. Beijing no longer talks of liberating Taiwan but of its reunification with the motherland. Meanwhile, Taiwan no longer talks of reconquering the mainland but of unifying all China under the political philosophy of the Three People's Principles of Dr. Sun Yat-sen.

Beijing considers the reunification a top priority of the 1980s, of equal importance with socialist modernization and continued opposition to Soviet hegemonism. To this end, it has offered a reunification plan based on three principles: (1) the Nationalist government must give up all claim to being the legal government of all China; (2) Taiwan may retain its present economic and social system and its standard of living; and (3) Taiwan may retain a degree of autonomy including the maintenance of an army. To begin the reconciliation, on New Year's Day 1979 Beijing proposed postal, commercial, and air and shipping relations with Taiwan. Then, a day before National Day on October 1, 1981, Marshal Ye Jianying intensified the peace offensive with a nine-point proposal:[9]

1. In order to bring an end to the unfortunate separation of the Chinese nation as early as possible, we propose that talks be held between the Communist Party of China and the Kuomintang of China on a reciprocal basis so that the two parties will cooperate for the third time to accomplish the great cause of national reunification. The two sides may first send people to meet for an exhaustive exchange of views.

2. It is the urgent desire of the people of all nationalities on both sides of the Straits to communicate with each other, reunite with their relatives, develop trade and increase mutual understanding.

   We propose that the two sides make arrangements to facilitate the exchange of mails, trade, air and shipping services, and visits by relatives and tourists as well as academic, cultural and sports exchanges, and reach an agreement thereupon.

3. After the country is reunified, Taiwan can enjoy a high degree of autonomy as a special administrative region and

it can retain its armed forces. The central government will not interfere in local affairs on Taiwan.

4. Taiwan's current socio-economic system will remain unchanged; so will its way of life and its economic and cultural relations with foreign countries. There will be no encroachment on the proprietary right and lawful right of inheritance on private property, houses, land and enterprise, or on foreign investments.

5. People in authority and representative personages of various circles in Taiwan may take up posts of leadership in national political bodies and participate in running the state.

6. When Taiwan's local finances are in difficulty, the central government may subsidize it according to the circumstances.

7. For people of all nationalities and public figures of various circles in Taiwan who wish to come and settle on the mainland, it is guaranteed that proper arrangements will be made for them, that there will be no discrimination against them, and that they will have the freedom of entry and exit.

8. Industrialists and businessmen in Taiwan are welcome to invest and engage in various economic undertakings on the mainland, and their legal rights, interests and profits are guaranteed.

9. The reunification of the motherland is the responsibility of all Chinese. We sincerely welcome people of all nationalities, public figures of all circles and all mass organizations in Taiwan to make proposals and suggestions regarding affairs of state through various channels and in various ways.

It is noteworthy that Ye calls for talks between the two ruling parties rather than between governments, sidestepping the sensitive question of which legitimately governs all China. However, the proposal seems as much directed at Taiwan as at others. The first five points would appeal to world, especially American, public opinion, while the sixth, suggesting that the mainland is in a position to assist Taiwan financially, seems designed for domestic consumption—it has perhaps the much needed psychological effect of lifting the party prestige before the one billion people of China. The peace offensive also coincides with a strong diplomatic move to pressure the United States not to sell sophisticated defense weapons such as the F5E fighter to Taiwan—a sale which Beijing insists would stiffen the resistance of Taiwan.

On October 9 and 10, 1981, a grand celebration was held at the Great Hall of the People to honor the seventieth anniversary of the 1911 Republican Revolution, on which occasion party Chairman Hu Yaobang made a persuasive appeal to Taiwan. He took note of the failure of the two earlier collaborations between the two parties (1923–27, 1937–41) but suggested that past experience need not deter one from trying again: "We do not wish to settle old accounts here. Let bygones be bygones. Let the lessons of the past help us cooperate better in the future." Hu proposed removing barriers of longstanding animosity and building mutual trust anew through contact and talk. Capitalizing on traditional Chinese respect for the deceased, Hu announced that Dr. Sun's mausoleum and Chiang Kai-shek's ancestral tombs are in good repair and invited Taiwan leaders to come see for themselves. "Doesn't Mr. Chiang Ching-kuo love his native land? Doesn't he want to have Mr. Chiang Kai-shek's remains moved back and buried in the Chiang family cemetery in Feng-hua?" Hu assured Taiwan leaders that they would be warmly welcomed whether they wished to talk or not and asked what they have to lose by doing so. A third cooperation between the parties, said Hu, would let Dr. Sun rest in peace.[10]

In conjunction with this speech, October 1981 saw a major campaign to honor Dr. Sun as the great revolutionary forerunner who made possible the later successful struggles of the Chinese people. By placing his portrait prominently in Tian An Men Square, by reprinting his *Complete Works*, by exhibiting his memorabilia and pictures of his life, and by holding an international academic conference in Wuhan to commemorate the 1911 revolution, the Communists hope to claim legitimacy as Sun's loyal followers, thereby establishing some common ground for initiating negotiations with the Nationalists.

Certainly it is Beijing's strategy to appear reasonable and magnanimous to the world, especially the United States. But the nine-point proposal in essence asks the Nationalists, in the larger interest of reunification, to forfeit their de facto independence and their claim to legitimacy as representative of the Chinese people, to cease to be a separate entity in world politics, and to accept the lesser status of an autonomous special region of China on a par with other provinces.

President Chiang Ching-kuo has adamantly refused to respond to the peace overture as a "smiling diplomacy" of the "United Front" variety designed to weaken the will of the people on Taiwan and to discredit his government in world opinion. Taiwan accuses the Communists of "usurping" the legacy of Dr. Sun and warns that the peace offensive could be a prelude to the infiltration and even the military invasion of the island. Cooperation is possible, says Taiwan, only if Beijing gives up communism in favor of the Three People's Principles and free enterprise.

Taiwan's continuous boycott of peace talks places it unfavorably in international light; it is tantamount to losing the propaganda war by default. Yet it is a calculated risk Taiwan is willing to take in the firm belief that negotiating with the Communist government is utterly futile. Any breakthrough is made the more difficult by Beijing's insistence on the four basic principles of the socialist line, the proletarian dictatorship, the leadership of the Communist party, and Marxism-Leninism and the Thought of Mao. These would rule out any meaningful participation by the Nationalists in any coalition government.

Moreover, the economic and political systems of the two places are so different that neither could absorb the other. With a $300 per capita annual income, the mainland economy is unattractive to those on Taiwan who enjoy free enterprise and an income eight times higher. The terms of the peace offensive ask Taiwan to contribute its considerable talents and resources to the modernization of a communist state. If experts from Taiwan did participate in the economic development of the mainland, certain capitalist elements would inevitably erode the present communist system and ultimately destabilize it.

It would take an enormous sacrifice and adjustment on both sides to achieve even a semblance of cooperation. Realistically, conditions do not seem ripe now. However, the prospects for reunion will improve in the future as China becomes more technocratic and less doctrinaire and Taiwan more flexible. Beijing already has shown some signs of liberalization. *Hongqi* [Red flag], the theoretical journal of the Communist party, ran an article urging "party democracy" to protect people's rights to "elect, criticize, supervise, and recall" party officials[11] —terms remarkably close to the four rights of the Three People's Principles: election, recall, initiative, and referendum. But of course "party democracy" can be interpreted in different ways.

A hundred years ago leaders of the Self-strengthening Movement sought "wealth and power" as the key to China's survival in the modern world. During the May Fourth Movement (1919) survival dictated national independence and unity, science and democracy, liberty and improvement of people's livelihood. Later the demand for freedom of thought and for the liberation of the creative spirit of man appeared.[12] Clearly, any government that could fulfill these aspirations would have the support of all Chinese.

In its 4,000 years of recorded history, China had been divided and reunited countless times. If history is any guide, and if politics is the art of expecting the unexpected, then one need not lose heart over the present difficulties. The genius of the Chinese people will find a way to make all China one again.

NOTES

1. *Free China Weekly,* Dec. 16, 1979.
2. *The Christian Science Monitor,* editorial, July 20, 1980. In the United States, 9 to 1; in Mexico, 20 to 1.

3. *A Review of Public Administration: The Republic of China,* compiled by the Administrative Research and Evaluation Commission, Executive Yuan, 1975, (Taipei, 1975), pp. 79–80, 96.
4. In 1979–80, there were 17,560 students from Taiwan enrolled in United States colleges and universities, next only to Iran's 51,310. Other large foreign student groups are: Nigeria, 16,360; Canada, 15,130; Japan, 12,260; and Hong Kong, 9,900. See *The Chronicle of Higher Education,* May 11, 1981, p. 14.
5. US Department of State, "Review of Relations with Taiwan," Current Policy No. 190, June 11, 1980 (Washington, D.C.).
6. *Central Daily News,* April 13, 1981.
7. *Central Daily News,* editorial, May 28, 1981.
8. Shao Yü-ming, "Wo-men tsou na-t'iao lu" (Which way shall we go?), *Hai-wai hsüeh-jen* [Overseas scholars], No. 101, Dec. 1980, p. 15.
9. *China Daily,* Beijing, Oct. 1, 1981.
10. Hu Yaobang, "Speech at Beijing Rally for 70th Anniversary of 1911 Revolution." Delivered at Great Hall of the People, Oct. 9, 1981.
11. *Hongqi* [Red flag], No. 17, Sept. 1980, p. 3.
12. Shao Yü-ming, "Shih-lun Chung-Kung cheng-ch'uan tsai Chung-kuo chin-tai-shih shang ti kung-kuo," (An appraisal of the achievements and failures of the Chinese Communist regime in modern Chinese history), *Hai-wai hsüeh-jen* [Overseas scholars], No. 99, Oct. 1980, p. 8.

FURTHER READING

A Review of Public Administration: The Republic of China, compiled by the Administrative Research and Evaluation Commission, Executive Yuan (Taipei, 1975).

Chen Hsi-en, Theodore, "Taiwan's Future," *Current History,* 77: 449:71–73, 83–84 (Sept. 1979).

Clough, Ralph, *Island China* (Cambridge, Mass., 1978).

Cohen, Myron L., *House United, House Divided: The Chinese Family in Taiwan* (New York, 1976).

Department of State, "Diplomatic Relations with the People's Republic of China and Future Relations with Taiwan" (Washington, D.C., Dec. 1978).

———, "Review of Relations with Taiwan," Current Policy No. 190 (Washington, D.C., June 11, 1980).

Economic Development: Taiwan, Republic of China, compiled by the Council for Economic Planning and Development, (Taipei, May 1979).

Faurot, Jeannette I. (ed.), *Chinese Fiction from Taiwan* (Bloomington, 1980).

Ho, Samuel P. S., *Economic Development of Taiwan, 1860–1970* (New Haven, 1978).

Hsü, Paul S. P., "The Uses of Taiwan in the Developing World," *Sino-American Relations,* VI:1:19–27 (Spring 1981).

Huang, Mab, *Intellectual Ferment For Political Reforms in Taiwan, 1971–1973* (Ann Arbor, 1976).

Jacobs, J. Bruce, "A Preliminary Model of Particularistic Ties in Chinese Political Alliances: *Kan-ch'ing* and *kuan-hsi* in a Rural Taiwanese Township," *The China Quarterly,* 78:237–73 (June 1979).

Knapp, Ronald G. (ed.), *China's Island Frontier: Studies in the Historical Geography of Taiwan* (Honolulu, 1981).

Lai, T. C., *Three Contemporary Chinese Painters: Chang Da-chien, Ting Yin-yung, Ch'eng Shih-fa* (Seattle, 1976).

Lau, Joseph S. M., and Timothy A. Ross (eds.), *Chinese Stories from Taiwan, 1960–1970* (New York, 1976).

Lee, Teng-hui, "Goals and Strategies for Taipei City," *Sino-American Relations,* VI:1:3–8 (Spring 1980).

Lerman, Arthur Jay, *Taiwan's Politics: The Provincial Assemblyman's World* (Washington, D.C., 1978).

Li, Victor H. (ed. with intro.), *The Future of Taiwan: A Difference of Opinion* (White Plains, N.Y., 1980).

Lin, Zili, "Shehui zhuyi di xueshuo yu shijian" (The theory and practice of socialism), *Renmin Ribao* [People's daily], Beijing, April 16, 1981.

Nickun, James E., and David C. Schak, "Living Standards and Economic Development in Shanghai and Taiwan," *The Chinese Quarterly,* 77:25–49 (March 1979).

Shao, Yü-ming, "Wo-men tsou na-t'iao lu" (Which way shall we go?), *Hai-wai hsüeh-jen* [Overseas scholars], 101:11–16 (Dec. 1980).

Silin, Robert H., *Leadership and Values: The Organization of Large-Scale Taiwanese Enterprises* (Cambridge, Mass., 1976).

Tien, Hung-mao, "Uncertain Future: Politics in Taiwan," in Robert B. Oxnam and Richard C. Bush (eds.), *China Briefing, 1980* (Boulder, 1980), pp. 87–99.

Guide to Pinyin and Wade-Giles Systems

Pinyin	*Wade-Giles*
Ah Jia	Ah Chia
Baoshan	Pao-shan
Beijing	Peking
Bo Ibo	Po I-po
Chai Zemin	Ch'ai Tse-min
Chen Boda	Ch'en Po-ta
Chen Xilian	Ch'en Hsi-lien
Chen Yonggui	Ch'en Yung-kuei
Chen Yun	Ch'en Yün
Chengdu	Ch'eng-tu
Daqing	Ta-ch'ing
Dazhai	Ta-chai
Deng Xiaoping	Teng Hsiao-p'ing
Diaoyu tai	Tiao-yü-t'ai
Ding Sheng	Ting Sheng
Fei Xiaotong	Fei Hsiao-t'ung
gong nong bing	kung-nung-ping
Guangming Ribao	*Kuang-ming Jih-pao*
Guangzhou	Canton
Hai Rui	Hai Jui
He Long	Ho Lung
Hu Qiaomu	Hu Ch'iao-mu
Hu Yaobang	Hu Yao-pang
Hua Guofeng	Hua Kuo-feng

Huang Hua	Huang Hua
Huang Huoqing	Huang Huo-ch'ing
Huang Kecheng	Huang K'e-ch'eng
Huang Zhen	Huang Chen
Ji Dengkui	Chi Teng-k'uei
jia tian xia	*chia-t'ien-hsia*
jia zhang zhi	*chia-chang-chih*
Jiang Hua	Chiang Hua
Jiang Qing	Chiang Ch'ing
Jiang Wen	Chiang Wen
Jidong	Chi-tung
Kang Sheng	K'ang Sheng
Li Dazhao	Li Ta-chao
Li Xiannian	Li Hsien-nien
Liang Xiao	Liang Hsiao
Liao Mosha	Liao Mo-sha
Lin Biao	Lin Piao
Liu Huaqing	Liu Hua-ch'ing
Liu Shaoqi	Liu Shao-ch'i
Lu Dingyi	Lu Ting-i
Mao Yuanxin	Mao Yüan-hsin
Mao Zedong	Mao Tse-tung
Nanjing	Nanking
Peng Chong	P'eng Ch'ung
Peng Dehuai	P'eng Te-huai
Peng Zhen	P'eng Chen
pingfan	*p'ing-fan*
Qinghua	Tsinghua
Qu Qiubai	Ch'ü Ch'iu-pai
Qun yan tang	*Ch'ün-yen-t'ang*
Shaanxi	Shensi
Shenyang	Shen-yang
Sichuan	Szechwan
Su Yu	Su Yü
Su Zhenhua	Su Chen-hua

Tangshan	T'ang-shan
Tao Zhu	T'ao Chu
Tian An Men	Tien-an-men
Tianjin	Tientsin
tianzai renhuo	*t'ien-tsai jen-huo*
tiyong	*t'i-yung*
Wang Dongxing	Wang Tung-hsing
Wang Hairong	Wang Hai-jung
Wang Hongwen	Wang Hung-wen
Wang Renzhong	Wang Jen-chung
Wang Zhen	Wang Chen
Wei Guoqing	Wei Kuo-ch'ing
Wu De	Wu Te
Wu Zetian	Wu Tse-t'ien
xiafang	*hsia-fang*
Xie Fuzhi	Hsieh Fu-chih
Xu Shiyou	Hsü Shih-yu
Xu Xiangqian	Hsü Hsiang-ch'ien
Yang Deze	Yang Te-tse
Yang Jingren	Yang Ching-jen
Yao Wenyuan	Yao Wen-yüan
Yao Yilin	Yao I-lin
Ye Jianying	Yeh Chien-yin
yi qiong er bai	*i-ch'iung erh-pai*
Yi yan tang	*I-yen-t'ang*
Yu Huiyong	Yü Hui-yung
Yu Qiuli	Yü Ch'iu-li
Zhang Aiping	Chang Ai-p'ing
Zhang Chunqiao	Chang Ch'un-ch'iao
Zhang Jingfu	Chang Ching-fu
Zhao Cangbi	Chao Ts'ang-pi
Zhao Ziyang	Chao Tzu-yang
Zhongfa	Chung-fa
Zhongnanhai	Chung-nan-hai
Zhou Enlai	Chou En-lai
Zhu De	Chu Teh
zhufan	*chu-fan*
Zunyi	Tsunyi

Appendix

On Questions of Party History

—Resolution on Certain Questions in the History of Our People Since the Founding of the People's Republic of China

(Adopted by the Sixth Plenary Session of the Eleventh Central Committee of the Communist Party of China on June 27, 1981)

THE DECADE OF THE "CULTURAL REVOLUTION"

19. The "cultural revolution," which lasted from May 1966 to October 1976, was responsible for the most severe setback and the heaviest losses suffered by the Party, the state and the people since the founding of the People's Republic. It was initiated and led by Comrade Mao Zedong. His principal theses were that many representatives of the bourgeoisie and counter-revolutionary revisionists had sneaked into the Party, the government, the army and cultural circles, and leadership in a fairly large majority of organizations and departments was no longer in the hands of Marxists and the people; that Party persons in power taking the capitalist road had formed a bourgeois headquarters inside the Central Committee which pursued a revisionist political and organizational line and had agents in all provinces, municipalities and autonomous regions, as well as in all central departments; that since the forms of struggle adopted in the past had not been able to solve this problem, the power usurped by the capitalist-roaders could be recaptured only by carrying out a great cultural revolution,

Extract from "On Questions of Party History," *Beijing Review*, No. 27, July 6, 1981.

by openly and fully mobilizing the broad masses from the bottom up to expose these sinister phenomena; and that the cultural revolution was in fact a great political revolution in which one class would overthrow another, a revolution that would have to be waged time and again. These theses appeared mainly in the May 16 Circular, which served as the programmatic document of the "cultural revolution," and in the political report of the Ninth National Congress of the Party in April 1969. They were incorporated into a general theory— of continued revolution under the dictatorship of the proletariat"—which then took on a specific meaning. These erroneous "Left" theses, upon which Comrade Mao Zedong based himself in initiating the "cultural revolution," were obviously inconsistent with the system of Mao Zedong thought, which is the integration of the universal principles of Marxism-Leninism with the concrete practice of the Chinese revolution. These theses must be thoroughly distinguished from Mao Zedong Thought. As for Lin Biao, Jiang Qing and others, who were placed in important positions by Comrade Mao Zedong, the matter is of an entirely different nature. They rigged up two counter-revolutionary cliques in an attempt to seize supreme power and, taking advantage of Comrade Mao Zedong's errors, committed many crimes behind his back, bringing disaster to the country and the people. As their counter-revolutionary crimes have been fully exposed, this resolution will not go into them at any length.

20. The history of the "cultural revolution" has proved that Comrade Mao Zedong's principal theses for initiating this revolution conformed neither to Marxism-Leninism nor to Chinese reality. They represent an entirely erroneous appraisal of the prevailing class relations and political situation in the Party and state.

1. The "cultural revolution" was defined as a struggle against the revisionist line or the capitalist road. There were no grounds at all for this definition. It led to the confusing of right and wrong on a series of important theories and policies. Many things denounced as revisionist or capitalist during the

"cultural revolution" were actually Marxist and socialist principles, many of which had been set forth or supported by Comrade Mao Zedong himself. The "cultural revolution" negated many of the correct principles, policies and achievements of the seventeen years after the founding of the People's Republic. In fact, it negated much of the work of the Central Committee of the Party and the People's Government, including Comrade Mao Zedong's own contribution. It negated the arduous struggles the entire people had conducted in socialist construction.

2. The confusing of right and wrong inevitably led to confusing the people with the enemy. The "capitalist-roaders" overthrown in the "cultural revolution" were leading cadres of Party and government organizations at all levels, who formed the core force of the socialist cause. The so-called bourgeois headquarters inside the Party headed by Liu Shaoqi and Deng Xiaoping simply did not exist. Irrefutable facts have proved that labelling Comrade Liu Shaoqi a "renegade, hidden traitor and scab" was nothing but a frame-up by Lin Biao, Jiang Qing and their followers. The political conclusion concerning Comrade Liu Shaoqi drawn by the Twelfth Plenary Session of the Eighth Central Committee of the Party and the disciplinary measure it meted out to him were both utterly wrong. The criticism of the so-called reactionary academic authorities in the "cultural revolution" during which many capable and accomplished intellectuals were attacked and persecuted also badly muddled up the distinction between the people and the enemy.

3. Nominally, the "cultural revolution" was conducted by directly relying on the masses. In fact, it was divorced both from the Party organizations and from the masses. After the movement started, Party organizations at different levels were attacked and became partially or wholly paralyzed, the Party's leading cadres at various levels were subjected to criticism and struggle, inner-Party life came to a standstill, and many activists and large numbers of the basic masses whom the Party has long relied on were rejected. At the beginning of the "cultural revolution," the vast majority of participants in

the movement acted out of their faith in Comrade Mao Zedong and the Party. Except for a handful of extremists, however, they did not approve of launching ruthless struggles against leading Party cadres at all levels. With the lapse of time, following their own circuitous paths, they eventually attained a heightened political consciousness and consequently began to adopt a sceptical or wait-and-see attitude towards the "cultural revolution," or even resisted and opposed it. Many people were assailed either more or less severely for this very reason. Such a state of affairs could not but provide openings to be exploited by opportunists, careerists and conspirators, not a few of whom were escalated to high or even key positions.

4. Practice has shown that the "cultural revolution" did not in fact constitute a revolution or social progress in any sense, nor could it possibly have done so. It was we and not the enemy at all who were thrown into disorder by the "cultural revolution." Therefore, from beginning to end, it did not turn "great disorder under heaven" into "great order under heaven," nor could it conceivably have done so. After the state power in the form of the people's democratic dictatorship was established in China, and especially after socialist transformation was basically completed and the exploiters were eliminated as classes, the socialist revolution represented a fundamental break with the past in both content and method, though its tasks remained to be completed. Of course, it was essential to take proper account of certain undesirable phenomena that undoubtedly existed in Party and state organisms and to remove them by correct measures in conformity with the Constitution, the laws and the Party Constitution. But on no account should the theories and methods of the "cultural revolution" have been applied. Under socialist conditions, there is no economic or political basis for carrying out a great political revolution in which "one class overthrows another." It decidedly could not come up with any constructive program, but could only bring grave disorder, damage and retrogression in its train. History has shown that the "cultural revolution," initiated by a leader laboring under a misapprehension and

capitalized on by counter-revolutionary cliques, led to domestic turmoil and brought catastrophe to the Party, the state and the whole people.

21. The "cultural revolution" can be divided into three stages.

1. From the initiation of the "cultural revolution" to the Ninth National Congress of the Party in April 1969. The convening of the enlarged Political Bureau meeting of the Central Committee of the Party in May 1966 and the Eleventh Plenary Session of the Eighth Central Committee in August of that year marked the launching of the "cultural revolution" on a full scale. These two meetings adopted the May 16 Circular and the Decision of the Central Committee of the Communist Party of China Concerning the Great Proletarian Cultural Revolution respectively. They launched an erroneous struggle against the so-called anti-Party clique of Peng Zhen, Luo Ruiqing, Lu Dingyi and Yang Shangkun and the so-called headquarters of Liu Shaoqi and Deng Xiaoping. They wrongly re-organized the central leading organs, set up the "Cultural Revolution Group Under the Central Committee of the Chinese Communist Party" and gave it a major part of the power of the Central Committee. In fact, Comrade Mao Zedong's personal leadership characterized by "Left" errors took the place of the collective leadership of the Central Committee, and the cult of Comrade Mao Zedong was frenziedly pushed to an extreme. Lin Biao, Jiang Qing, Kang Sheng, Zhang Chunqiao and others, acting chiefly in the name of the "Cultural Revolution Group," exploited the situation to incite people to "overthrow everything and wage full-scale civil war." Around February 1967, at various meetings, Tan Zhenlin, Chen Yi, Ye Jianying, Li Fuchun, Li Xiannian, Xu Xiangqian, Nie Rongzhen and other Political Bureau Members and leading comrades of the Military Commission of the Central Committee sharply criticized the mistakes of the "cultural revolution." This was labeled the "February adverse current," and they were attacked and repressed. Comrades Zhu De and Chen Yun were also wrongly criticized. Almost all leading Party and government departments in the different spheres

and localities were stripped of their power or re-organized. The chaos was such that it was necessary to send in the People's Liberation Army to support the Left, the workers and the peasants and to institute military control and military training. It played a positive role in stabilizing the situation, but it also produced some negative consequences. The Ninth Congress of the Party legitimatized the erroneous theories and practices of the "cultural revolution," and so reinforced the position of Lin Biao, Jiang Qing, Kang Sheng and others in the Central Committee of the Party. The guidelines of the Ninth Congress were wrong, ideologically, politically and organizationally.

2. From the Ninth National Congress of the Party to its Tenth National Congress in August 1973. In 1970-71 the counter-revolutionary Lin Biao clique plotted to capture supreme power and attempted an armed counter-revolutionary coup d'etat. Such was the outcome of the "cultural revolution" which overturned a series of fundamental Party principles. Objectively, it announced the failure of the theories and practices of the "cultural revolution." Comrades Mao Zedong and Zhou Enlai ingeniously thwarted the plotted coup. Supported by Comrade Mao Zedong, Comrade Zhou Enlai took charge of the day-to-day work of the Central Committee and things began to improve in all fields. During the criticism and repudiation of Lin Biao in 1972, he correctly proposed criticism of the ultra-Left trend of thought. In fact, this was an extension of the correct proposals put forward around February 1967 by many leading comrades of the Central Committee who had called for the correction of the errors of the "cultural revolution." Comrade Mao Zedong, however, erroneously held that the task was still to oppose the "ultra-Right." The Tenth Congress of the Party perpetuated the "Left" errors of the Ninth Congress and made Wang Hongwen a vice-chairman of the Party. Jiang Qing, Zhang Chunqiao, Yao Wenyuan and Wang Hongwen formed a gang of four inside the Political Bureau of the Central Committee, thus strengthening the influence of the counter-revolutionary Jiang Qing clique.

3. From the Tenth Congress of the Party to October 1976.

Early in 1974 Jiang Qing, Wang Hongwen and others launched a campaign to "criticize Lin Biao and Confucius." Jiang Qing and the others directed the spearhead at Comrade Zhou Enlai, which was different in nature from the campaign conducted in some localities and organizations where individuals involved in and incidents connected with the conspiracies of the counter-revolutionary Lin Biao clique were investigated. Comrade Mao Zedong approved the launching of the movement to "criticize Lin Biao and Confucius." When he found that Jiang Qing and the others were turning it to their advantage in order to seize power, he severely criticized them. He declared that they had formed a gang of four and pointed out that Jiang Qing harbored the wild ambition of making herself chairman of the Central Committee and "forming a cabinet" by political manipulation. In 1975, when Comrade Zhou Enlai was seriously ill, Comrade Deng Xiaoping, with the support of Comrade Mao Zedong, took charge of the day-to-day work of the Central Committee. He convened an enlarged meeting of the Military Commission of the Central Committee and several other important meetings with a view to solving problems in industry, agriculture, transport and science and technology, and began to straighten out work in many fields so that the situation took an obvious turn for the better. However, Comrade Mao Zedong could not bear to accept systematic correction of the errors of the "cultural revolution" by Comrade Deng Xiaoping and triggered the movement to "criticize Deng and counter the Right deviationist trend to reverse correct verdicts," once again plunging the nation into turmoil. In January of that year, Comrade Zhou Enlai passed away. Comrade Zhou Enlai was utterly devoted to the Party and the people and stuck to his post till his dying day. He found himself in an extremely difficult situation throughout the "cultural revolution." He always kept the general interest in mind, bore the heavy burden of office without complaint, racking his brains and untiringly endeavoring to keep the normal work of the Party and the state going, to minimize the damage caused by the "cultural revolution" and to protect many Party and non-Party cadres. He waged all forms of struggle to counter sabotage by the counter-revolutionary Lin Biao and Jiang Qing cliques. His death left the whole Party and people in the most profound grief. In April of the same year, a powerful movement of protest signalled by the Tian An Men Incident swept the whole country, a movement to mourn for the late Premier Zhou Enlai and oppose the gang of four. In essence, the movement was a demonstration of support for the Party's correct leadership as represented by Comrade Deng Xiaoping. It laid the ground for massive popular support for the subsequent overthrow of the counter-revolutionary Jiang Qing clique. The Political Bureau of the Central Committee and Comrade Mao Zedong wrongly assessed the nature of the Tian An Men Incident and dismissed Comrade Deng Xiaoping from all his posts inside and outside the Party. As soon as Comrade Mao Zedong passed away in September 1976, the counter-revolutionary Jiang Qing clique stepped up its plot to seize supreme Party and state leadership. Early in October of the same year, the Political Bureau of the Central Committee, executing the will of the Party and the people, resolutely smashed the clique and brought the catastrophic "cultural revolution" to an end. This was a great victory won by the entire Party, army and people after prolonged struggle. Hua Guofeng, Ye Jianying, Li Xiannian and other comrades played a vital part in the struggle to crush the clique.

22. Chief responsibility for the grave "Left" error of the "cultural revolution," an error comprehensive in magnitude and protracted in duration, does indeed lie with Comrade Mao Zedong. But after all it was the error of a great proletarian revolutionary. Comrade Mao Zedong paid constant attention to overcoming shortcomings in the life of the Party and state. In later years, however, far from making a correct analysis of many problems, he confused right and wrong and the people with the enemy during the "cultural revolution." While making serious mistakes, he repeatedly urged the whole Party to study the works of Marx, Engels and Lenin conscientiously and imagined that his theory and practice were Marxist and that they were essential for the consolidation of the dictatorship

of the proletariat. Herein lies his tragedy. While persisting in the comprehensive error of the "cultural revolution," he checked and rectified some of its specific mistakes, protected some leading Party cadres and non-Party public figures and enabled some leading cadres to return to important leading posts. He led the struggle to smash the counter-revolutionary Lin Biao clique. He made major criticisms and exposures of Jiang Qing, Zhang Chunqiao and others, frustrating their sinister ambition to seize supreme leadership. All this was crucial to the subsequent and relatively painless overthrow of the gang of four by our Party. In his later years, he still remained alert to safeguarding the security of our country, stood up to the pressure of the social-imperialists, pursued a correct foreign policy, firmly supported the just struggles of all peoples, outlined the correct strategy of the three worlds and advanced the important principle that China would never seek hegemony. During the "cultural revolution" our Party was not destroyed, but maintained its unity. The State Council and the People's Liberation Army were still able to do much of their essential work. The Fourth National People's Congress which was attended by deputies from all nationalities and all walks of life was convened and it determined the composition of the State Council with Comrades Zhou Enlai and Deng Xiaoping as the core of its leadership. The foundation of China's socialist system remained intact and it was possible to continue socialist economic construction. Our country remained united and exerted a significant influence on international affairs. All these important facts are inseparable from the great role played by Comrade Mao Zedong. For these reasons, and particularly for his vital contributions to the cause of the revolution over the years, the Chinese people have always regarded Comrade Mao Zedong as their respected and beloved great leader and teacher.

24. In addition to the above-mentioned immediate cause of Comrade Mao Zedong's mistake in leadership, there are complex social and historical causes underlying the "cultural revolu-

tion" which dragged on for as long as a decade. The main causes are as follows:

1. The history of the socialist movement is not long and that of the socialist countries even shorter. Some of the laws governing the development of socialist society are relatively clear, but many more remain to be explored. Our Party had long existed in circumstances of war and fierce class struggle. It was not fully prepared, either ideologically or in terms of scientific study, for the swift advent of the newborn socialist society and for socialist construction on a national scale. The scientific works of Marx, Engels, Lenin and Stalin are our guide to action, but can in no way provide ready-made answers to the problems we may encounter in our socialist cause. Even after the basic completion of socialist transformation, given the guiding ideology, we were liable, owing to the historical circumstances in which our Party grew, to continue to regard issues unrelated to class struggle as its manifestations when observing and handling new contradictions and problems which cropped up in the political, economic, cultural and other spheres in the course of the development of socialist society. And when confronted with actual class struggle under the new conditions, we habitually fell back on the familiar methods and experiences of the large-scale, turbulent mass struggle of the past, which should no longer have been mechanically followed. As a result, we substantially broadened the scope of class struggle. Moreover, this subjective thinking and practice divorced from reality seemed to have a "theoretical basis" in the writings of Marx, Engels, Lenin and Stalin because certain ideas and arguments set forth in them were misunderstood or dogmatically interpreted. For instance, it was thought that equal right, which reflects the exchange of equal amounts of labor and is applicable to the distribution of the means of consumption in socialist society, or "bourgeois right" as it was designated by Marx, should be restricted and criticized, and so the principle of "to each according to his work" and that of material interest should be restricted and criticized; that small production would continue to engender capitalism

and the bourgeoisie daily and hourly on a large scale even after the basic completion of socialist transformation, and so a series of "Left" economic policies and policies on class struggle in urban and rural areas were formulated; and that all ideological differences inside the Party were reflections of class struggle in society, and so frequent and acute inner-Party struggles were conducted. All this led us to regard the error in magnifying class struggle as an act in defence of the purity of Marxism. Furthermore, Soviet leaders started a polemic between China and the Soviet Union, and turned the arguments between the two Parties on matters of principle into a conflict between the two nations, bringing enormous pressure to bear upon China politically, economically and militarily. So we were forced to wage a just struggle against the big-nation chauvinism of the Soviet Union. In these circumstances, a campaign to prevent and combat revisionism inside the country was launched, which spread the error of broadening the scope of class struggle in the Party, so that normal differences among comrades inside the Party came to be regarded as manifestation of the revisionist line or of the struggle between the two lines. This resulted in growing tension in inner-Party relations. Thus it became difficult for the Party to resist certain "Left" views put forward by Comrade Mao Zedong and others, and the development of these views led to the outbreak of the protracted "cultural revolution."

2. Comrade Mao Zedong's prestige reached a peak and he began to get arrogant at the very time when the Party was confronted with the new task of shifting the focus of its work to socialist construction, a task for which the utmost caution was required. He gradually divorced himself from practice and from the masses, acted more and more arbitrarily and subjectively, and increasingly put himself above the Central Committee of the Party. The result was a steady weakening and even undermining of the principle of collective leadership and democratic centralism in the political life of the Party and the country. This state of affairs took shape only gradually and the Central Committee of the Party should be held partly responsible. From the Marxist viewpoint, this complex phenome-

non was the product of given historical conditions. Blaming this on only one person or on only a handful of people will not provide a deep lesson for the whole Party or enable it to find practical ways to change the situation. In the communist movement, leaders play quite an important role. This has been borne out by history time and again and leaves no room for doubt. However, certain grievous deviations, which occurred in the history of the international communist movement owing to the failure to handle the relationsip between the Party and its leader correctly, had an adverse effect on our Party, too. Feudalism in China has had a very long history. Our Party fought in the firmest and most thoroughgoing way against it, and particularly against the feudal system of land ownership and the landlords and local tyrants, and fostered a fine tradition of democracy in the anti-feudal struggle. But it remains difficult to eliminate the evil ideological and political influence of centuries of feudal autocracy. And for various historical reasons, we failed to institutionalize and legalize inner-Party democracy and democracy in the political and social life of the country, or we drew up the relevant laws but they lacked due authority. This meant that conditions were present for the overconcentration of Party power in individuals and for the development of arbitrary individual rule and the personality cult in the Party. Thus, it was hard for the Party and state to prevent the initiation of the "cultural revolution" or check its development.

Index

Ah Jia, 135–36

Bo Ibo, appointed vice premier, 36; signs four agreements in Washington, D.C., 81

Brown, Harold, visits China, 82; speaks of "shared interest" against U.S.S.R., 82–83; offers high technology, 83; sees Chinese air and naval shows, 83; believes Chinese military technology generally 25–30 years behind, 83

Brzezinski, Zbigniew, to China, May 1978, 59; warmly welcomed by Chinese, 59; echoes China's world view, 59; jokes with Chinese about the "polar bear," 60; reveals to Chinese two secret documents, 60; Chinese consider his visit "two steps forward," 60

Carter, Jimmy, President, favors normalization, 57; in no hurry to move, 58; wants to look decisive in China matter, 61; sets Jan. 1, 1979, as deadline for recognition of China, 61; orders Ambassador Leonard Woodcock to negotiate with Chinese, 61–62; announces diplomatic recognition of China on Dec. 15, 1978, 62; his move supported by majority of Americans, 63; terms of diplomatic recognition, 63–64; move approved by the press, 65; attacked by Ronald Reagan and Barry Goldwater, 65; sued by Goldwater and associates, 66; sends delegation under Warren Christopher to Taiwan to explain action, 66; complex American ties with Taiwan, 67; continued arms sales to Taiwan, 67

Chai Zemin, Chinese ambassador, received by Carter, 61; given conditions of Sino-American normalization of relations, 61

Chen Boda, at trial, 135; plots the death of Liu Shaoqi, 135; presses false charge against Zhu De, 135; given eighteen years' imprisonment, 138

Chen Xilian, supports Hua Guofeng, 14; removal from Politburo, 39

Chen Yonggui, resigns as vice premier, 41

Chen Yun, appointed vice premier, 36; on assessment of Mao, 128; does not want to make Jiang Qing a revolutionary martyr, 138

Chiang Ching-kuo, inaugurated president of the National Government on Taiwan, 60; angered by U.S. recognition of Beijing, 66; emphasizes self-reliance and dignity in the face of international adversity, 67; promotes major projects on Taiwan, 174–75; elected chairman of the Nationalist Party in 1975, 177; elected president of the Nationalist Government in 1978, 178; his work-style different from his father's, 178; selects many Taiwanese to join his government, 178; character of his administration, 178; ignores Beijing's 9-point peace proposal, 183

Chinese communism, a 30-year review, 158–67; vital statistics of population, GNP, and productions, 161–64

Collective leadership of Deng-Hu-Zhao, 43, 147

Cultural Revolution, the "decade of catastrophe," 6, 52; value negated, 40; condemned at the trial of the Gang of Four, 130; must not be allowed to recur, 142; completely negated by the party, 147–50

Daqing oil field, losses "paragon" status, 49

Dazhai commune, loses "model" status, 49

Democracy Wall, 38

Deng Xiaoping, groomed by Zhou Enlai as his successor, 6; disappears after Zhou's memorial services on Jan. 15, 1976, 6, dismissed from all offices, 8; secret plotting against the Gang of Four, 14; rehabilitation, 30–31; appointed party vice chairman, 32; conflict with Hua Guofeng, 33; enlargement of power base, 34; introduces "young blood," 35, 39; pronounces

"Practice is the sole criterion of truth," and "Seek truth from facts," 35; promotes "Economics in Command," 38; idea of a new "collective leadership," 41, 43, 147; policy of retiring aging cadres, 41; more successful than Mao in solving succession problem, 43; expresses wish to visit U.S.A., 62; receives Woodcock in Dec. 1978 and formalizes normalization of relations with the U.S., 62; achieves what eluded Mao and Zhou, 64; needs U.S. cooperation in China's modernization and in confronting the U.S.S.R., 65; visit to the U.S., 70; captivates American public and law makers, 72–73; speaks mildly on Taiwan, 71; attacks U.S.S.R., 71–72; wants to read Vietnam "lessons," 72; tours the U.S. and sees democracy and capitalistic enterprises at work, 72–73; signs 3 agreements, 73; pronounces visit a "complete success," 73; promotes Four Modernizations, 92–93; calls National Science Conference, 93; named chairman of the CCP Military Commission, 147

Eleventh Party Congress, August 12–18, 1977, 32; signals the beginning of the end of the Maoist era, 32

Fang Yi, in charge of development of science and technology, 33; appointed president of Chinese Academy of Sciences, 36; appointed to party secretariat, 39

Ford, Gerald, President, 57

Four Basic Principles, 156

Four Modernizations (of industry, agriculture, science and technology, and national defense), aims of, 91; first proposed by Zhou Enlai, 91; promoted by Deng Xiaoping, 93; announcement by Yu Qiuli, 43; high targets of the Ten-Year Plan, 93–100; cost of, 101; problems of, 101–6; retrenchment of, 106–8; probable achievement targets for 1985, 109; new interest in profit, 110; material incentive and structural reorganization, 110–12; consequences of rapid modernization, 113–16; inadequate planning of Baoshan steel complex, 113; opposed by the Gang of Four, 117–18; a "Chinese styled" modernization, 118; cultural consequences, 118; a great revolution in itself, 157

Gang of Five, 140

Gang of Four, 3; members of, 13; manipulations for succession to Mao and Zhou, 13; claims Mao's support through his "deathbed adjuration," 15; lured into false security, 16; smashed on Oct. 6, 1976, 18; reasons for failure, 20; charges against, 21; condemned by the party, 31–32; oppose foreign technology, 117–18, trial of, 126ff

Goldwater, Barry, sues President Carter over legality of recognizing China, 66; loses suit at court, 69

Haig, Alexander, to China in June 1981 to discuss increased arms sales and greater military cooperation, 84–85

Hu Qiaomu, president of Chinese Academy of Social Sciences, favors adoption of advanced Western science and technology to accelerate China's modernization, 49; calls for realism in Four Modernizations, 107

Hu Yaobang, 35–36; appointed to Politburo Standing Committee, 39; made head of party secretariat, 39; on assessment of Mao, 128; named chairman of the CCP, 147; proposes peace talk with KMT, 182

Hua Guofeng, appointed acting premier, 6; lacks power base, 7; attacked by Liang Xiao, 7; given three instructions by Mao on April 30, 1976, 8; declares Mao's "Three do's and don't's" to counter the Gang, 8; takes charge of the smashing of the Gang, 14, 16–18; appointed chairman of the party and premier, 18; legality of his appointment questioned, 18–19, 29–30; reasons for his success, 20; willing to consider Deng's rehabilitation, 30; approved as party chairman in July 1977, 31; delicate relationship with Deng, 36; resigned as premier, 41; branded a "whateverist," 49; announces normalization of relations with U.S., 63–64; promotes Four Modernizations, 92; unveils the Ten-Year Plan, 93;; implicated by Jiang Qing at the trial, 127; difficult position at the trial, 128–29; pre-trial manipulation, 129; excused from the trial of the Gang of Four, 129; party assessment of, 148

Huang Hua, appointed vice premier, 41; signs agreements with U.S., 73

Huang Huoqing, 131, reads indictment of the Gang of Four and Lin Biao group, 131

Ji Dengkui, removed from office, 38

Jiang Qing, *see* Gang of Four; at trial, 126; protests her innocence, 127; blames Mao for all her actions, 127; defiant at trial, 130;

plays a Chinese "Joan of Arc," 132; accused of framing Zhou Enlai and blocking Deng's appointment as premier, 132; plots the death of Liu Shaoqi, 135; given a 2-year suspended death sentence, 138

Jiang Wen, on Mao's responsibility in the Cultural Revolution and the crimes of Lin Biao and Jiang Qing, 137

Kang Sheng, condemned, 21; would have been prosecuted if alive, 131; plots the purge and death of Liu Shaoqi, 135
Kreps, Juanita, 79

Legal procedure in China, different from that of the West, 139–40
Li Dazhao, 146, 151
Li Xiannian, appointed to Politburo Standing Committee and party vice chairman, 32
Liao Mosha, imprisoned by Jiang Qing for 8 years, 135
Lin Biao group at trial, 126, 129–31, 135, 138
Liu Shaoqi, restored to honor posthumously, 39; his widow (Wang Guangmei) rehabilitated, 48, 53; praised by Deng, 48; given high assessment by Ye Jianying, 51; praised by Hu Yaobang, 151

Mao Yuanxin, connection with Jiang Qing, 17; arrested, 18
Mao Zedong, 3; failing health of, 9; China's Lenin and Stalin combined, 10; brief comments on his life, 10–12; "deathbed adjuration," 15; relations with the Gang of Four, 22–25; knows his wife's "wild ambitions," 25; Arthur Miller's comments on, 25; his thought subject to scrutiny, 35; infallibility denied, 40; de-sanctified, 44–51; warns against overemphasis on material progress, 92; promotes industrialization in the 1950s, 116; separated from the trial of the Gang of Four, 128; held responsible for the catastrophe of the Cultural Revolution, 137; trial of the Gang an indirect indictment of, 140; assessment by General Huang, 143–45; party assessment of, 147–48; Hu Yaobang's assessment, 149–50; a historian's assessment, 151–54; reasons for his enormous power and patriarchal rule, 154–55

Mondale, Walter, joke with Deng, 71; visits China in Aug. 1979 to reassure the Chinese of American friendship and to offer $2 billion aid, 80; signs 2 agreements, 80–81

Nixon, President, 56; Watergate prevents him from recognizing China, 57; needs conservative support, 57

Normalization of relations with the U.S., three Chinese conditions, 56; Taiwan proves obstacle to Sino-American rapprochement and becomes an issue in American domestic politics, 57

October 6, 1976, coup, 16

Peng Chong, 39

Peng Dehuai, restored to honor, 48; listed as a historically outstanding person, 146; praised by Hu Yaobang, 151

Peng Zhen, 35

Pingfan (righting the wrong), 34

Press, Dr. Frank, visits China in July 1978, 61

Qu Qiubai, 146, 151

Reagan, Ronald, criticizes Carter for recognizing China, 65; arms sales, 84–85

Shieh Tung-ming, vice president on Taiwan, 178

Sino-American joint communiqué on diplomatic normalization, 63–64

Sino-American trade agreements, 81–82

Taiwan, shocked by U.S. recognition of People's Republic of China, 66; struggle for some form of official relations with U.S., 66; self-reliance, 67–68; creation of a Coordinating Council for North American Affairs in Washington, D.C. to replace the embassy, 8; American Institute in Taipei, 68; Taiwan Relations Act, 68; economic progress, 172; high standard of living, 173; economic strategy, 174; 10 major projects, 174; Export Processing Zones, 175–76; foreign and overseas Chinese investments, 176; consequences of rapid industrialization, 177; population density, 177; Palace Museum, 177–78; "great country of tomorrow," 179; rejects Beijing's three conditions for reunification, 180; refuses to respond to Marshal Ye's 9-point peace proposal, 183; difficulties of reconciliation, 183–84

Tang, Nancy, 132

Tangshan earthquake, 3, 9

Tao Zhu, restored to honor, 48

Tian An Men Square Incident, April 1976, 7; linked by Beijing Mayor Wu De to the "Antirightist Deviationist Campaign," 7; verdict on, reversed, 48

Ulanfu, 35

Vance, Cyrus, visits China, Aug. 1977, 58; Chinese consider his visit "a step backward," 59
Vietnam, signs treaty of alliance with U.S.S.R., 69; invasion of Cambodia, 69; attacked by Deng in the U.S. 72; invaded by the Chinese in Feb. 1979, 73; Chinese aid to, 74; Chinese want quick success but cannot get it, 75–76; China learns a "lesson" about modern warfare, 78

Wan Li, appointed executive vice premier, 43
Wang Dongxing, Mao's bodyguard in charge of the "8341" unit, 14; role in smashing the Gang of Four, 17; reports on the arrest of the Four, 18; appointed to Politburo Standing Committee, 14; appointed party vice chairman, 32; under attack, 35; fall from power, 38; exempted from the trial of the Gang of Four, 129
Wang Guangmei, 48, 53
Wang Hairong, 132
Wang Hongwen, at trial, 127, 129, 132; warned by Mao not to "hang around with Jiang Qing," 135; given life sentence, 138
Wu De, and Tian An Men Incident, 3; came under attack, 35; fall from power, 38

Xie Fuzhi, 131

Yang Deze, 39
Yang Jingren, 41
Yao Wenyuan, his article on "Hai Rui" rejected, 48; at trial, 126, 128; given 20 years' imprisonment, 138
Yao Yilin, appointed vice premier, 36
Ye Jianying, masterminds the smashing of the Gang, 14; reports to the Politburo on the smashing of the Gang of Four, 18; appointed party vice chairman, 32; appointed chairman of the National People's Congress, 33; criticizes Mao on the 30th anniversary of the founding of the People's Republic, 50–51; proposes a 9-point reunification plan with Taiwan, 180–81

Yenan, left in benign neglect as a revolutionary shrine of the past, 49

Yu Qiuli, appointed chairman of State Planning Commission, 33; appointed to party secretariat, 39; announcement on Four Modernizations, 92–93

Zhang Aiping, General, 41

Zhang Chunqiao, attacks Hua Guofeng, 7; at trial, 127; given a 2-year suspended death sentence, 138

Zhang Jingfu, settles "frozen assets and blocked claims" with Juanita Kreps, 78; negotiates a trade pact giving China most-favored-nation treatment in the U.S., 79

Zhao Cangbi, 32

Zhao Ziyang, appointed to Politburo Standing Committee, 39; appointed premier, 41; his "economic miracle" in Sichuan, 43; part of top collective leadership, 156

Zhou Enlai, death, 3; brief comments on his life and career, 4–6; initiating the idea of Four Modernizations, 91; listed as a historically great man, 146; praised by Hu Yaobang, 151

Zhu De, death, 3; considered a historically outstanding person, 146; praised by Hu Yaobang, 151